# 2 to 22
# AROUND
# THE GREAT LAKES

THE ITINERARY PLANNER
1991 Edition

ARNOLD SCHUCHTER

John Muir Publications
Santa Fe, New Mexico

Other JMP travel guidebooks by Arnold Schuchter
*The Shopper's Guide to Art and Crafts in the
    Hawaiian Islands*
*22 Days in Hawaii*
*2 to 22 Days in New Zealand*

John Muir Publications, P.O. Box 613, Santa Fe, NM 87504

© 1991 by Arnold Schuchter
Cover map © 1991 by John Muir Publications
All rights reserved. Published 1991
Printed in the United States of America

First edition. First printing

Library of Congress Cataloging-in-Publication Data
Schuchter, Arnold (Arnold L.)
    2 to 22 Days Around the Great Lakes  :  the itinerary plan-
ner  /  Arnold Schuchter. — 1st ed.
        p.   cm.
    Includes index.
    ISBN 0-945465-62-9
    1. Great lakes Region—Description and travel—Tours.
I. Title. II. Title: Two to twenty-two days around the Great
Lakes.
F551.S58    1991
917.704'33—dc20                                              90-24867
                                                                         CIP


Distributed to the book trade by:
W. W. Norton & Company, Inc.
New York, New York


**Typeface** Garamond Light
**Maps** Jim Wood
**Cover Map** Michael Taylor
**Typography** Copygraphics, Inc., Santa Fe, N. Mex.
**Printer** McNaughton & Gunn, Inc., Saline, Mich.

# CONTENTS

# 2 to 22 Days Around the Great Lakes

LAKE SUPERIOR

Pictured Rocks Pk.
Munising
Sault St. Marie
St. Ignace
Escanaba
Mackinac Island
Fayette
Mackinaw City
Menominee
DOOR PENINSULA
31
Grayling
LAKE HURON
Green Bay
Oshkosh
GRAND TRAVERSE
LAKE MICHIGAN
Wisconsin Dells
Baraboo
Bay City
Port Huron
Niagara Falls
51
Madison
Flint
69
Sarnia
Buffalo
Spring Green
Milwaukee
401
Ann Arbor
Detroit
South Haven
94
Kalamazoo
Windsor
LAKE ERIE
Chicago

N

# HOW TO USE THIS BOOK

Three of the states visited in this itinerary—Illinois, Wisconsin, and Michigan—are bound together by two of the vast and beautiful Great Lakes, Michigan and Superior. You'll touch Lake Huron at only two points, St. Ignace/ Mackinac Island and Port Huron, possibly before entering Ontario and skirting Lake Erie en route to Niagara Falls. The different natural and man-made environments among the Great Lakes—farms and forests, villages, towns, and cities—are dotted with smaller bodies of water: Glen Lake, North and South Higgins lakes, and thousands of other lakes; the Fox, Wolf, Peshtigo, Au Sable, Niagara, and other rivers and streams; man-made waterways such as the Welland Canal between Lakes Erie and Ontario and waterfalls of the Wisconsin Dells, Pictured Rocks National Lakeshore, and the grandest of all, Niagara.

The Great Lakes region is a land of contrasts, ranging from big cities to villages and towns to large national and state forests to hundreds of miles of lakefront. The area seems huge, but the driving distances actually are not that great: Chicago is less than 300 miles from Detroit and 600 miles from Niagara, and Milwaukee is 115 miles from Green Bay.

The 22 days presented in this itinerary are **modules** that you can piece together in any combination that works for you. For example:

- start and end the trip anywhere
- skip a day or several days
- stay in one place as long as you like
- follow the seasons and reverse the suggested itinerary (such as starting in the Upper Peninsula in fall and following the fall southward, or heading east to Ontario and then northwest to Michigan in spring)
- spend a day or several days on one activity, such as fishing, bicycling, cross-country skiing, visiting museums and attending festivals, or beachcombing.

This book guides you along a route through parts of three Great Lakes states (Illinois, Wisconsin, and Michigan) and across southwestern Ontario in Canada. The route starts in Chicago and heads north. But you could start anywhere along the route or in neighboring states, for example, from Niagara Falls and Buffalo westward or Minneapolis eastward or northward from Indianapolis. Wherever you decide to enter the planned route and whichever direction you decide to travel, you'll know how much driving and sightseeing you can do comfortably for any destinations in the *22 Days* itinerary.

The itinerary format for each day contains:

1. A **suggested schedule** for each day's travel and sightseeing.
2. Detailed **transportation** and driving directions.
3. **Descriptive overviews** and **sightseeing highlights**, rated in order of importance: ▲▲▲ Don't miss; ▲▲ Try hard to see; ▲ See if you get a chance.
4. **Restaurant, lodging, nightlife**, and **shopping** recommendations.
5. **Itinerary options**—excursions, adventures, and outdoor recreation suggestions, some of which require more time than the suggested schedule. Others are mainly for people with special interests.
6. **Maps** of the region, specific city, or area covered in the text, which are intended to be easier to read and to use than typical road maps.

First read the "Itinerary" sections below in order to understand the way in which the *2 to 22 Days Around the Great Lakes* itinerary is put together. Then look at the day-by-day schedules to see specific suggestions for things to see and do. Be sure to also read the Itinerary Options for each day. Together, the Sightseeing Highlights and the Itinerary Options cover most of the things that are worth seeing and doing in each area.

You may find that some itinerary options include attractions and activities that are even more interesting to you than the suggested sightseeing highlights. The reason is that many itinerary options take too much time to fit into the *22 Days* itinerary. In fact, an entire Great Lakes itinerary can't possibly fit into 22 days. This book includes one extended itinerary option, to Niagara Falls, which adds three days to the 22 days described below.

**When to Travel**

Most people will prefer to travel to the Great Lakes during May through September. Late spring, summer, and early fall are the best times to arrive in Chicago to experience the most comfortable weather. The chart below shows the minimum and maximum temperatures to expect while traveling May through September in the region.

### Chicago, Northern and Southern Michigan Maximum/Minimum Daily Average Temperatures (in degrees Fahrenheit)

|                  | May   | June  | July  | Aug.  | Sept. |
|------------------|-------|-------|-------|-------|-------|
| Chicago          | 65/50 | 75/60 | 81/66 | 79/65 | 73/58 |
| Green Bay         | 59/43 | 68/52 | 77/60 | 75/58 | 66/51 |
| Escanaba          | 58/42 | 69/53 | 76/59 | 74/57 | 65/50 |
| Munising          | 59/41 | 70/51 | 76/58 | 74/58 | 66/50 |
| Sault Ste. Marie  | 60/38 | 70/47 | 76/53 | 74/53 | 64/46 |
| Leland            | 65/44 | 76/55 | 81/60 | 80/59 | 72/51 |
| Higgins Lake      | 66/42 | 75/51 | 79/53 | 77/53 | 68/47 |
| Detroit           | 69/48 | 79/59 | 84/64 | 82/63 | 74/55 |

The week before Memorial Day is an excellent time to arrive in Chicago and the Great Lakes to see attractions that open between May 1 and Memorial Day and to enjoy springtime. Remember that many attractions around the northern Great Lakes are seasonal and do not open until Memorial Day. By the end of May, spring will be in full bloom in Door County, Wisconsin's north woods, the Upper Peninsula, and the Grand Traverse area of north-western Michigan. If you arrive in Chicago in early fall, no later than mid-September when the temperature is in the low 70s, you can follow the fall in its grandest intensity around the Great Lakes.

## Lodging and Camping

Wisconsin and Michigan have an abundance of excellent and reasonably priced motels, hotels, inns, and especially B&Bs. Obtain a free copy of *Michigan's Bed & Breakfast and Historic Inns* from the Travel Bureau, Michigan Department of Commerce. For accommodations outside the major cities, my suggestions focus on exceptional public and private campgrounds and also B&Bs because of their amenities, ambience, good value, and wonderful innkeepers, many of whom I've met as I have traveled around the Great Lakes.

Because of the popularity of certain state parks during summer (the Wisconsin Dells, Door Peninsula, Big Bay on Madeline Island, J. W. Wells, Tahquamenon Falls, Straits, Petoskey, Traverse City, Leelanau, Interlochen, North Higgins Lake, and others), reservations are a must between the fourth week of June and Labor Day. Campsites with electrical hookups are especially scarce in state parks during this period.

In Wisconsin, there are three levels of camping fees in state parks for nonresidents, ranging from $6.75 to $10 per night. Residents pay between $4 and $6 per night. Electricity $1.75 extra. A reservation fee of $3 is charged. The daily vehicle admission fee is $3.50 for residents and $6 for nonresidents. You may purchase an annual admissions sticker at $30 for nonresidents and $14 for residents, which is available at the state parks. In Michigan, an annual vehicle sticker for unlimited entry into all state parks is $10. Campground fees range from $4 to $9 per night. Michigan has many more state parks with campgrounds than Wisconsin does.

All Wisconsin campsite reservations have to be made on reservation forms available at state park and forest headquarters, Wisconsin's Tourist Information Centers in the state and Chicago, and State Division of Natural Resources Headquarters (see below). In Michigan, make telephone and in-person reservations at any park office or directly with the particular parks. Application forms also are available at Michigan Division of Natural Resource regional and district offices, the Information Service Center in Lansing, or the Michigan Travel Bureau in Lansing (see below).

Throughout the Great Lakes, the nightly rate for recreation vehicles averages $12 a couple with hookups and $10 without hookups. This rate goes as low as $9 without hookups and as high as $29 with hookups. Two dollars for each child is not unusual. Check-out time is usually noon, and check-in is no later than 10:00 a.m. All of the private campgrounds recommended in this book have showers.

The Michigan Association of Private Campgrounds, P.O. Box 68, Williamsburg, MI 49690, publishes a free *Michigan Campground Directory* covering private parks, state parks and forests, national forests, county, municipal, and township parks with camping permitted, and recreational vehicle services. The Wisconsin Association of Campground Owners, P.O. Box 1770, Eau Claire, WI 54702, (715) 839-WACO, will send you its free *Wisconsin Annual Campground Directory*.

**Recommended Reading**
The best information for travel planning is free from state tourism and natural resource protection and development agencies. Contact: Illinois Office of Tourism, 310 S. Michigan Avenue, Chicago, IL 60604, (312) 793-2094; Michigan Travel Bureau, 333 S. Capitol Avenue, Town Center Building, Suite F, Lansing, MI 48933, (800) 543-2937; Wisconsin Division of Tourism, Box 7606, Madison, WI 53707, (800) 432-TRIP, and the Wisconsin Department of Tourism Development, Box 7606, Madison, WI 53707, (608) 266-2161; The Ontario Department of Tourism, Queens Park, Toronto, Ontario, M7A 2E5, Canada, (800) 268-3735; and Niagara County Tourism, 59 Park Avenue, Lockport, NY 14094, (800) 338-7890.

The Wisconsin Department of Natural Resources, Bureau of Parks and Recreation, P.O. Box 7921, Madison, WI 53707, provides a free map of *Wisconsin State Parks*. The Michigan Department of Natural Resources, Parks Division, Box 30028, Lansing, MI 48909, offers the *Michigan State Parks*.

Each state publishes a listing or calendar of cultural events and attractions. Write the Wisconsin Arts Board, 131 W. Wilson Street, Suite 301, Madison, WI 53702, (608) 266-0190. Also ask for their annual directory of arts and crafts fairs. A comparable directory is published by the Michigan Council for the Arts, 1200 Sixth Avenue, Executive Plaza, Detroit, MI 48226, (313) 256-3731.

*A Guide to Wisconsin Historic Sites* is published annually by the State Historical Society of Wisconsin, 816 State St., Madison, WI 53706. Comparable information is available from the Michigan Historical Museum, 717 West Allegan Street, Lansing, MI 48918, (517) 373-3559, and the Michigan Department of Natural Resources, (517) 373-1270.

A profusion of agricultural fairs and special events in Michigan is listed in a brochure provided by the Michigan Association of Fairs & Exhibitions, 1120 W. State Fair, Detroit, MI 48203, (313) 892-2520. The Wisconsin Department of Tourism Development has a free 70-page publication, *Wisconsin Calendar of Events*, giving listings of special events in every community.

*Wisconsin Trails* magazine, available monthly at newsstands for $3.95 (Wisconsin Tails and Trails, 6225 University Ave., Madison, WI 53705, $19 subscription) is a valuable source of information about Wisconsin's vacation meccas. Also see their *Best Wisconsin Bike Trails, 30 Best One-Day Trips*, by Phil Van Valkenberg ($9.95), the bible of bike trips in Wisconsin; and two books on the best canoeing rivers in Wisconsin, *Best Canoe Trails of Northern Wisconsin* and *Canoe Trails of Southern Wisconsin*, by Michael Duncanson.

Don Davenport has put together *A Traveler's Guide to Wisconsin State Parks & Forests*, published by the Bureau of Parks and Recreation, Wisconsin Department of Natural Resources (P.O. Box 7921, Madison, WI 53707, $10.95 with tax). Tom Powers's *Michigan State and National Parks* (Friede Publications, 2339 Venezia Dr., Davison, MI 48423, 1989) is well worth the $13.95 price for travelers planning to visit many of Michigan's outstanding state parks. My bible for Michigan's hiking, cross-country skiing, and all-terrain bicycle trails is Dennis R. Hansen and Danforth Holley's *Michigan Trail Atlas* (Hansen Publishing Company, 1801 Birchwood Dr., Okemos, MI 48864, June 1988, $19.95).

The *Wisconsin Recreation Guide* published by the Wisconsin Department of Tourist Development lists the most well known canoeing rivers as well as bicycle tour companies, boat tours, brewery and winery tours, charter fishing and sailing companies, cheese factory tours, horseback riding stables, houseboat vacations, fishing and hunting information sources, farm vacations, and watercraft rentals from rowboats to jet skis. Also included are the names, addresses, and telephone numbers of regional, county, and community tourism agencies. Be sure to ask for this guide.

Fishing the lakes, rivers, and streams for more than 50 species of fish is one of the main reasons for coming to the Great Lakes. Subscribe to six issues of *Michigan Natural Resource Magazine* and get *The Angler's Guide to Michigan's Great Lakes*, both for $9.97 (*Michigan Natural Resource Magazine*, Box 30034, Lansing, MI 48909). From the Division of Natural Resource's Wildlife Division, get a copy of the *Michigan Hunting* and *Trapping Guide* for license and hunting rules. For information on hunting and hunting conditions, call the wildlife newsline, (517) 373-WILD, a tape-recorded message played 14 hours a day.

The route of *2 to 22 Days Around the Great Lakes* touches Lake Michigan at two points, the waterfronts of Chicago and Milwaukee, before heading inland through central Wisconsin to scenic Door Peninsula. From Green Bay, it cuts across Michigan's Upper Peninsula to some of Lake Superior's finest coastal scenery and the trip's halfway mark at Pictured Rocks National Lakeshore. After crossing two straits, at Sault Ste. Marie and Mackinac, it returns to Lake Michigan along its northeastern shores to Sleeping Bear Dunes National Lakeshore. Turning inland through central Michigan to Detroit, it returns westward to Lake Michigan again and follows the curve of the lake back to Chicago.

Travelers with less time can plan shorter tours of some highlights. One of the best times to take short tours is the fall, when summer weather continues as the lakes slowly give up their warmth, apple and grape harvests are in full swing, leaves are turning vermilion and gold, salmon are running, and there's plenty of room in campgrounds and other accommodations at off-season prices. Here are some suggestions:

• Chicago to Milwaukee, Madison, Devil's Lake, Baraboo, the Wisconsin Dells, and beautiful Door County in seven days.
• Chicago to South Haven for a weekend, or add Ann Arbor and Detroit for a seven-day trip.
• Detroit to Grand Traverse, Leelanau Peninsula, and Mackinac Island in seven days, or to Niagara Falls and back in six days.
• St. Ignace along U.S. 2 to Escanaba, then down Highway 35 to Menominee.
• Highway 22 from Frankfort to Northport to Traverse City, then up Old Mission Peninsula.
• Madison to Mt. Horeb, east to Dodgeville, north to Spring Green and back to Madison on Highway 14 through Black Earth.

**DAY 1** Arrive in Chicago and aim for the Windy City's Miracle Mile—pulsating Michigan Avenue with more than 300 specialty shops between the Wrigley Building on the Chicago River and the John Hancock Tower. After lunch, bring the heavens closer at Chicago's planetarium. At the huge new Shedd Aquarium, monsters of the deep and a coral reef are just a few bubbles away. After dinner, enjoy the blues, ethnic festivities, or other nighttime entertainment.

**DAY 2** Across the street from the Shedd Aquarium, explore the vast natural history collection at the Field Museum until lunch. Go to the north side of the Loop where ten-mile-long Lincoln Park starts. Visit the zoo and its outstanding ape collection. Just a few minutes brisk walk takes you to the south end of the park and Chicago's Historical Society Museum. Dinner is followed by an evening of comedy in neighboring Old Town.

**DAY 3** Drive to Milwaukee and view its lakefront from the Milwaukee Art Museum. Drive downtown for a stroll on the Grand Avenue Mall and the red brick streets of Old World Third Street. A beer and bratwurst lunch gets you ready for a Pabst Brewery tour. Afterward, drive through Wisconsin's pasture and woodland to Madison, the state capital. After dinner, attend a theater performance on State Street or at the University of Wisconsin's Union Theater next to Lake Mendota.

**DAY 4** Visit the University of Wisconsin's Elvehjem Museum of Art and the State Capitol. Drive west to see folk art and antiques in a Mt. Horeb museum and, nearby, a collection of restored Scandinavian pioneer houses. Explore colorful limestone cave formations and the architecture of Frank Lloyd Wright's Taliesin. Cross a beautiful stretch of the Wisconsin River to Spring Green, gateway to a scenic valley meandering to magnificent bluffs overlooking Devil's Lake State Park.

**DAY 5** In Baraboo, just over the horizon from Devil's Lake, see the Ringling Bros. circus tents puffed with big-top fanfare next to the Circus World Museum. After lunch, visit the world's foremost collection of endangered crane species en route to the Wisconsin Dells and its astonishing assortment of man-made roadside attractions. Take a nighttime boat cruise on the Upper Dells.

**DAY 6** Drive from the Wisconsin Dells to Sturgeon Bay, gateway to Door Peninsula. In the home of Oshkosh B'Gosh, visit the EAA Air Adventure Museum. Save Green Bay for another day and let Sturgeon Bay help you to gear down for a slower pace on the scenic byways of Door Peninsula.

**DAY 7** Drive to quaintly named historic towns—Egg Harbor, Fish Creek, Ephraim, and Sister Bay—that hug the rugged Green Bay shoreline. Explore Potawatomi, Peninsula, Newport, or Whitefish Dunes state parks. Sightsee and shop in Fish Creek. Head up the Green Bay coast to Ellison Bay and Gill's Rock after lunch and down the opposite Lake Michigan coast through Rowley's Harbor, Bailey's Harbor, and Jacksonport to get back to Fish Creek in time for refreshments and a fish boil dinner.

**DAY 8** Drive from Fish Creek through Peninsula State Park and northward again to the Northport Pier Ferry Dock for the car ferry to Washington Island's Detroit Harbor. Explore Washington Island en route to the ferry to Rock Island State Park. Return to the peninsula for a leisurely dinner in Bailey's Harbor.

**DAY 9** Take in a 1762 fur trader's cabin in Green Bay's Heritage Hill State Park and the NFL history of Vince Lombardi's team in the Packer Hall of Fame. Drive along scenic Green Bay coastline to the Michigan border at Marinette/Menominee.

**DAY 10** Menominee's Waterfront Historic District and the Marinette County Logging Museum provide historical insight into this southern gateway to Michigan's Upper Peninsula. A scenic drive along M-35 leads to Escanaba. Drive farther along the Lake Michigan coast and the Bays de Noc and down the Garden Peninsula to visit the picturesque ghost town of Fayette in Fayette State Park.

**DAY 11** Drive to Kitch-iti-ki-pi, Michigan's largest spring-fed pond, and then across the Upper Peninsula to Munising. View the waterfalls in Pictured Rocks National Lakeshore before an evening cruise along the spectacular colored cliffs.

**DAY 12** Seeing Pictured Rocks National Lakeshore's beautiful waterfalls and stunning cliff overlooks fills most of the morning. Enjoy a relaxing picnic lunch on Twelve-mile Beach. In the afternoon, see Au Sable Light Station, magnificent Grand Sable Dunes, and Grand Marais's beach. Visit the Pictured Rocks Maritime Museum and the Historical Museum in Grand Marais, eastern gateway to Pictured Rocks. In the late afternoon, drive south to Seney National Wildlife Refuge for a tour of wetland wildlife. Stay overnight within easy reach of Tahquamenon Falls State Park.

**DAY 13** Close-ups of Lower Tahquamenon Falls and the more spectacular Upper Tahquamenon Falls are easily accessible from park pathways. Afterward, drive through Paradise to the Great Lakes Shipwreck Museum at scenic Whitefish Point. Drive to Sault Ste. Marie to view the Soo Locks from several vantage points. Delve into more Great Lakes maritime history at the Museum Ship Valley Camp before heading to St. Ignace for the evening.

**DAY 14** One of the frequent ferries from St. Ignace will take you back in time to Mackinac Island. On foot, in a horse-drawn carriage, or on a bicycle, tour Main Street's shops and restaurants and the rest of the island. See local history reenacted at Fort Mackinac. Splurge on dinner at the truly Grand Hotel—a highlight of the trip.

**DAY 15** Cross the Mackinac Bridge over the Straits of Mackinac to Mackinaw City. See restored Fort Michilimackinac's history brought to life by costumed interpreters and the Mackinac Maritime Museum. The scenic drive to Harbor Springs on M-119 brings you to the boating mecca of Harbor Springs and Petoskey's Gaslight District.

**DAY 16** From Traverse City, the hub of the Grand Traverse region and Michigan's cherry capital, drive up beautiful Old Mission Peninsula, which is covered with cherry trees. Then take the scenic roads and byways of Leelanau Peninsula. Visit wineries, craft shops, and the picturesque towns of Northport and Leland. Schedule dinner in Leland early enough to catch sunset from Fishtown wharf. Drive on to Glen Arbor and prepare for an early morning excursion to Sleeping Bear Dunes National Lakeshore.

**DAY 17** Dunes rise dramatically hundreds of feet from sandy shores along Lake Michigan to towering bluffs that you'll ascend on Pierce Stocking Drive. Clamber up a wall of sand covering Sleeping Bear for panoramic views of Glen Lake and the Manitou Islands. Leave this striking scene for central Michigan, passing the famous Interlochen Center for the Arts. Around Grayling, canoe or fish for trout in the fabled Au Sable River, in season hunt for delicious morel mushrooms, and enjoy the clean blue waters of North Higgins Lake. In Hartwick Pines State Park, see one of Michigan's last magnificent stands of white pine.

**DAY 18** Follow scenic I-75 south to Flint, with a side trip to Bavarian Frankenmuth, where you can enjoy its famous chicken. Visit one of Flint's fine cultural and art institutions before turning east to Port Huron, Thomas Edison's boyhood home. End the day at an exceptional B&B, the Victorian Inn.

**OPTIONAL EXTENSION: Port Huron— Niagara Falls—Detroit**

**DAY 19** In Port Huron, explore local history around the Blue Water Bridge before leaving for Detroit. Arriving in Detroit from Port Huron, Flint, or Ontario, experience the city's potent cultural and historical side first. Drive to the Detroit Institute of Arts for a guided tour and lunch. Then visit the Detroit Historical Museum. After dinner, attend a live performance at the splendid Fox Theater.

**DAY 20** During a morning on Belle Isle, visit a museum, aquarium, zoo, nature trail, and other attractions. Enjoy excellent views of downtown Detroit, the Detroit River, and Canada. Picnic on the island or have lunch in Rivertown on the way downtown to catch the Detroit People Mover. Swish on the monorail to colorful Greektown and adjoining Bricktown. After an early dinner, get ready for an evening of fine music or theater.

**DAY 21** Drive west to Ann Arbor for a leisurely tour of the University of Michigan's museums and historic Kerrytown's shopping and eating delights. Stroll around a downtown planned for enjoyable walking. Stay in town for dinner and an evening of entertainment.

**DAY 22** Break the drive to Lake Michigan in Kalamazoo, and arrive at the Idler Riverboat in South Haven in time for lunch. Before returning to Chicago, relish one last afternoon at a superb Lake Michigan beach in South Haven. Dinner is only a few steps from the beach. After dinner, there's still time for one last stroll on the beach before driving back to Chicago.

## CHICAGO

Whether you arrive at O'Hare Airport or Midway Airport or drive into the city, start the day where Michigan Avenue meets the lake at the northern tip of the Miracle Mile, near the John Hancock Tower. Work your way southward between Michigan Avenue and the lakefront, on foot or using buses or taxis, to the Navy Pier, Grant Park, the Aquarium, and the Planetarium. Spend the evening at one of the fabulous special events in Grant Park or elsewhere in town or capture the spirit of Chicago at a nightclub.

### Suggested Schedule

| | |
|---|---|
| 9:00 a.m. | Arrive in Chicago. |
| 10:00 a.m. | Visit Chicago Tourism Council. |
| 10:30 a.m. | See view from top of John Hancock Center. |
| 11:15 a.m. | See "Here's Chicago." |
| 11:45 a.m. | Lunch near the Water Tower. |
| 1:00 p.m. | Water Tower Shopping Center. |
| 2:00 p.m. | Taxi or bus to Adler Planetarium. Option: Museum of Contemporary Art. |
| 4:00 p.m. | Shedd Aquarium. |
| 6:00 p.m. | Return to hotel. |
| 7:00 p.m. | Dinner. |
| 8:30 p.m. | Attend a Grant Park event, or spend the evening at a blues or jazz club. |

### Transportation

You won't need a car for your two days in Chicago. From O'Hare International, 17 miles northwest of the Loop, **Continental Air Transport Company**, (312) 454-7800, operates buses from the airport to the Loop and 20 downtown hotels every 30 minutes from about 5:00 a.m. to 10:50 p.m. The fare is $9 one way and $15 round-trip. A taxi from O'Hare to downtown is about $20; a share-ride taxi costs $8. From **Midway Airport**, 9 miles southwest of the Loop, bus service is $7.50 one way and $13 round-trip. The Chicago Transport Authority (CTA) provides rapid transit to the Loop in 30 to 45 minutes for $1.

## Getting Around Chicago

Driving from O'Hare, follow signs to I-90 east to Chicago (Kennedy Expressway). This merges with I-94 (Edens Expressway). Exit eastbound on Ohio Street for Near North accommodations and Washington or Madison streets for Loop hotels. Drive straight east to reach Michigan Avenue and turn left to North Michigan—the Miracle Mile.

Chicago is laid out in a grid pattern. Streets run north-south or east-west. State Street is the east-west bisector, and Madison Street divides north from south. All addresses begin at this intersection. A uniform numbering system from this point makes it fairly easy to find an address. Downtown street numbers change by 100 every two blocks.

Street parking downtown is virtually nonexistent, and garage parking is very expensive. The city's public parking garages charge about $5 for eight hours. Private parking lots charge as much as $10 for eight hours or less. If you're renting a car, pick it up on your last evening in Chicago. Both Hertz, (312) 372-7600, and Avis, (312) 782-6825, have downtown locations. If you're driving your own car, leave it parked and use public transportation for touring the city.

Taxis are metered with a basic charge of $1 for the first tenth of a mile and $1 for each additional mile plus 50 cents for each additional person. Tip 10 percent of the meter reading. For quick response and good service, call a Yellow Cab, (312) 829-4222.

**The CTA** operates a network of bus, subway, and elevated (the "L") rapid transit lines radiating from the Loop. All fares are $1 plus 25 cents for a transfer. Exact change is required, and dollar bills are accepted. The CTA provides route information to callers—(312) 836-7000. Most hotels have city and CTA route maps. **The Chicago Tourism Council**, 163 East Pearson, (312) 280-5740, and the **State Street Tourist Council**, State and Madison, have maps and sightseers' guides.

## Chicago

De Palma's *The Untouchables* captured Chicago's Union Station and LaSalle Street. Davis's *Code of Silence* delivers great details of Uptown and Lower Wacker Drive, reinforced by Hyam's winterscape of Wacker Drive in *Running Scared* (understandably about people who desperately want to get out of Chicago in winter). But like the pool hall setting in *The Color of Money*, in films Chicago is alluring and dangerous but always undervalued and unreal.

Third largest city in the United States (following New York and Los Angeles), with a population of more than 3 million, Chicago sprawls 29 miles along Lake Michigan and 15 miles wide. Two branches of the Chicago River, "the river that flows backward," slice through the city. The river's flow was reversed in the late 1800s to keep sewage from polluting Lake Michigan. About the same time, a streetcar track was laid in a **Loop** that the elevated runs on today, bounded on the north and west by the Chicago River, on the south by Roosevelt Road, and on the east by Lake Shore Drive. Today, downtown Chicago, including the Loop, lies between Oak Street on the north, Congress to the south, Michigan Avenue and the lakefront to the east, and the Chicago River to the west.

Parallel to Michigan Avenue, **State Street** between Adams and Lake includes Chicago's oldest retail district. The grandest of all Chicago department stores, **Marshall Field's**, is at State and Washington and also at the newer Water Tower Place shopping center. LaSalle, Clark, and Dearborn streets between Jackson and Randolph streets contain the city's financial district, where the State of Illinois Building, City Hall, First National Bank Building and other banks, and countless law offices are located.

The only buildings to survive the Great Fire of 1871, the Water Tower and the Pumping Station, can be seen at

## Downtown Chicago

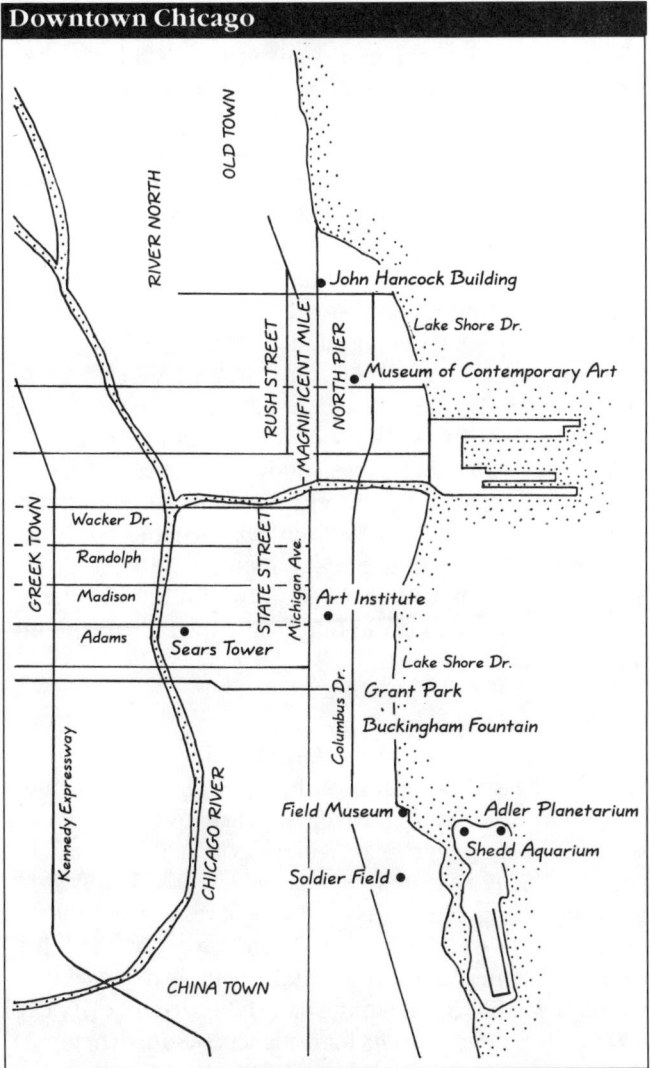

OLD TOWN

RIVER NORTH

John Hancock Building

Lake Shore Dr.

RUSH STREET

MAGNIFICENT MILE

NORTH PIER

Museum of Contemporary Art

GREEK TOWN

Wacker Dr.

Randolph

Madison

Adams

STATE STREET

Michigan Ave.

Art Institute

Sears Tower

Columbus Dr.

Lake Shore Dr.

Grant Park

Buckingham Fountain

Kennedy Expressway

CHICAGO RIVER

Field Museum

Adler Planetarium

Shedd Aquarium

Soldier Field

CHINA TOWN

Michigan and Pearson. These landmarks stand at the heart of Chicago's phenomenal retail and real estate development boom along North Michigan Avenue's "Miracle Mile."

Chicago's 11-story Home Insurance Company building (long gone) was the world's first skyscraper. Today, the city claims three of the world's five tallest buildings: the Sears Tower (1,454 feet), tallest in the world; the Amoco Building (1,136 feet), fourth tallest; and the John Hancock Center (1,127 feet), fifth tallest. The tallest bank in the world, the First National Bank Building, and the world's tallest residential building, Lake Point Tower, are also part of Chicago's collection of "tallest buildings."

Outside the business and financial district, a large part of the city is a mosaic of distinct ethnic neighborhoods, each with a unique heritage and personality. River North, the Gold Coast, Streeterville, Lincoln Park, Old Town, DePaul, New Town, and LakeView are in-town residential areas with interesting shops, restored old buildings, and a marvelous assortment of restaurants. Enclaves of most foreign nationalities dot the city. The Polish community stretching along Milwaukee Avenue is the largest outside of Warsaw. Other ethnic pockets include Chinatown along Wentworth Avenue, Greek Town on Halsted Street between Madison and Van Buren, and the Italian community along Taylor Street.

**Sightseeing Highlights**
▲▲▲ **Michigan Avenue's Miracle Mile**—From Oak Street's elegant boutiques south to the Michigan Avenue Bridge over the Chicago River, Michigan Avenue is lined with shops, art galleries, restaurants, office buildings, and famous Chicago landmarks. Near 900 North Michigan, with Bloomingdale's and five floors of restaurants and elegant shops, see the historic Water Tower and the John Hancock Center (see below). At the southern end of the Miracle Mile is the white Spanish Renaissance-style Wrigley Building, with its baroque terra-cotta ornamentation and clock tower, and the 1920s Gothic Tribune Tower.
▲▲▲ **Top of the city view point—John Hancock Center**'s skydeck observatory, 875 North Michigan Avenue, (312) 751-3680, is open daily from 9:00 a.m. to

midnight. Tickets are sold until 11:30 p.m. Admission is $3.50 for adults and $2.00 for children and senior citizens. Lines at the Hancock Center are shorter than at the Sears Tower.

▲▲ **Here's Chicago**—A multimedia exhibit, Michigan Avenue at Pearson, across the street from the Water Tower, (312) 467-7114, includes a 30-minute film on Chicago's history showing the Great Fire of 1871 and, naturally, Chicago's notorious gangster era. Open daily from 10:00 a.m. to 5:00 p.m. Adults $4.75, children $2, family $10.

▲▲ **The Illinois Tourist Information Office**— Located in the Historic Water Tower in the park adjacent to the Water Tower Shopping Center on Michigan Avenue, (312) 280-5740, this agency is a good source of city maps and tourist information brochures.

▲▲ **Navy Pier**—Head south on Michigan Avenue by bus or on foot to Grand Avenue, and take a left to the lake for one of the best views of Chicago's skyline. Open daily from 6:00 a.m. to 8:00 p.m. for fishing, Navy Pier, (312) 744-4219, is one of the best places to see special exhibits and entertainment. For example, in July and August, there are five ethnic festivals featuring music, arts, and crafts— Fiesta Italiana, Festival Polonaise, Irish Festival, PanAmerican Festival, and Viva Mexico.

▲▲▲ **Grant Park**—Extending from the Chicago River near Navy Pier south for several miles along Lake Shore Drive to Roosevelt Road, Grant Park is almost divided by the end of Congress Expressway, which aims at **Buckingham Fountain** on Lake Shore Drive. Made of red Georgia marble and surrounded by formal gardens, Buckingham Fountain is 280 feet at its greatest diameter, and the water in its central column rises 135 feet. Weather permitting, the fountain operates daily from Memorial Day to Labor Day from 11:30 a.m. to 9:00 p.m.

▲▲ **Adler Planetarium**—On a peninsula that juts a half-mile into Lake Michigan at the south end of Grant Park, the planetarium, 1300 Lake Shore Drive, (312) 322-0300, contains exhibits on astronomy, space exploration, telescopes, and navigation. The Sky Theater features multimedia shows (about 2 hours long) about the stars, planets, and distant galaxies. Open daily 9:30 a.m. to 4:30 p.m., with Friday night shows until 9 p.m. Admission to the planetarium is free, but Sky Theater tickets are $3 for adults and $1.50 for children 6 to 17.

▲▲ **The John G. Shedd Aquarium**—Just a little north of the planetarium, Chicago's "Ocean by the Sea," 1200 S. Lake Shore Drive, (312) 939-2438, contains more than 8,000 fresh water and saltwater creatures displayed in more than 200 naturalistic habitats. The Coral Reef Exhibit, for example, re-creates a Caribbean reef. The new oceanarium's huge saltwater tank is home to a pair of whales. During daily fish feedings at 11:00 a.m., 2:00 p.m., and 3:00 p.m., a diver talks to visitors and responds to questions through a two-way microphone. A full tour takes about 2 hours. Open from 9:00 a.m. to 5:00 p.m. daily from March through October and 10 a.m. to 5:00 p.m. from November through February. Admission is $2 for adults, $1 for children, 50 cents for senior citizens; no admission charge on Thursdays.

▲ **The Chicago Architecture Foundation**—For a schedule of walking tours of the Loop's historic architecture, call (312) 326-1393. Prices usually don't exceed $5 for a one-hour tour to see buildings designed by Louis Sullivan, Daniel Burnham, Frank Lloyd Wright, Mies van der Rohe, and Helmut Jahn and sculpture in street level and pedestrian plazas by Calder, Chagall, Picasso, Oldenberg, and others.

## Lodging

Since Chicago is a major convention center, weekday rates at hotels and inns often are high, and reservations may be difficult to obtain during late spring, summer, early fall, and December. Many hotels have weekend rates, but anticipate spending between $65 and $100 per night, and make reservations. Plan to arrive on a Friday night to take advantage of weekend rates at better hotels.

To get the most out of a short stay, even RVers should plan to stay in the city for two nights. Otherwise, at least three hours a day will be spent commuting to a campsite.

**Days Inn**, (800) 325-2525 or (312) 943-9200, overlooks the lake at 644 Lake Shore Drive and offers weekend rates. It's only four blocks from Oak Street Beach and the Miracle Mile at North Michigan Avenue and a nice half-mile walk to Lincoln Park.

**La Salle Motor Lodge**, 720 N. LaSalle Street, (312) 664-8100, and the **Ohio House Motel**, 600 N. LaSalle, (312) 943-6000, have rooms at $65 per night. Both offer free parking and are within a few blocks of North Michigan Avenue and within walking distance of many excellent restaurants. **The Inn of Chicago**, 162 E. Ohio at Michigan Avenue, (800) 528-1234, is a bargain with a weekend special of $59. The package includes complimentary cocktails, morning newspaper, and a welcome gift with advance reservations.

For B&B accommodations, contact **Bed and Breakfast Chicago Inc.**, P.O. Box 14088, Chicago, IL 60614, (312) 951-0085.

## Camping

**Illinois Beach State Park**, (312) 662-4811, about 35 miles north of Chicago on Sheridan and Wadsworth roads, has 276 campsites with electric hookups and showers for $9 per night. The campground adjoins seven miles of beautiful beach—Illinois' last natural lakeshore dunes area. From I-94, get off at the Highway 173/Zion exit, which also has an Illinois Beach State Park sign, and head east five miles. Follow signs to the park.

The closest KOA campground, the **Chicago Northwest KOA**, 8404 S. Union Road, Union, IL 60180, (815) 923-4206, is off I-90, 19 miles west of Elgin, or, if you're coming from the west on I-90, 26 miles east of Rockford. Take the Marengo exit and drive 4½ miles northwest on Highway 20 to South Union Road. Drive north for about 500 feet on S. Union Road. The basic rate is $15 plus $2.50 for electricity for two people. From the KOA, drive

12 ½ miles to the Woodstock station of the Chicago NW
Metro train, park free, ride downtown to Madison Street
(1¼ -hour trip; round-trip fare $11.25 per person), and
return by 11:00 p.m. or 2:00 a.m. Trains also run more fre-
quently from the Crystal Lake station, which is closer to
Chicago but a little longer drive. Next door is the seven-
acre **Antique Village Museum** with a large display of
old musical instruments, war weapons, and a western
town, with gunfights, of course. Only two miles away is
the **Illinois Railway Museum**, (800) 244-7245, with the
largest display of railroad equipment in the Midwest.
Admission at both places is about $5 adults.

**Food**
Ethnic neighborhoods offer authentic Old World cuisine
at fairly reasonable prices. Greek Town is just west of
downtown on Halsted Street and Jackson. A bit to the
south at Taylor, just west of Halsted, are several Italian
restaurants, some of which have been in the same location for more than 50 years. At Cermak and Wentworth,
Chinatown offers several excellent restaurants from small
carryout counters to grand dining rooms serving dim
sum or sumptuous buffets.

Early risers requiring more sustenance than a muffin
and coffee for breakfast should head for **Lou Mitchell's**,
565 W. Jackson, near Union Station, (312) 939-3111, for
light pancakes, French toast made of thick slices of fresh
bread, and omelets featuring cheese choices from ched-
dar to feta and fresh vegetable fillings. Open 5:30 a.m.
Monday through Saturday. The **Original Mitchell's**, 101
W. North Avenue, (312) 642-5246, owned by relatives of
Lou and within walking distance of the Gold Coast, Lincoln Park, and Old Town, serves similar generous portions; two can feast heartily for under $10.

**Cafe Delish**, 550 N. Wells Street, (312) 670-2600, is
within comfortable walking distance of North Michigan
Avenue to the east and River North art galleries to the

west. This bakery and restaurant serving breakfast and lunch from 7:00 a.m. to 4:00 p.m. also prepares wonderful carryout and picnic selections on fresh rolls, muffins, and croissants. Gourmet sandwiches are about $4.50. Ask about daily special soups and salads.

For lunch or dinner, try **Ed Debevic's**, 640 N. Wells, (312) 664-1707. This '50s-style diner is owned by famous Chicago restaurateur Rich Melman, who also owns a dozen other extremely successful restaurants all over Chicago. Ed's serves breakfast, burgers, meat loaf, pot roast, and good chili and features a blue plate special daily. Most lunch items are under $5. Kids will enjoy the music and theatrical waiters.

For German fare, definitely try **The Berghoff**, 17 West Adams, (312) 427-3170, a Chicago landmark serving veal, beef, pork, and fish items at reasonable prices, accompanied by memorably fresh dark rye. Open 11:00 a.m. to 9:30 p.m. Monday through Thursday and until 10:00 p.m. Friday and Saturday.

For tasty Chinese food, head for Chinatown and **Chiam**, 2323 S. Wentworth, (312) 225-6336, to indulge in a $10 dim sum feast served daily from 10:00 a.m. to 2:30 p.m.

Italian food fans should try the **Como Inn**, 546 N. Milwaukee, (312) 421-5222, open from 11:30 a.m. to 11:30 p.m. Monday through Saturday and from noon on Sunday. Lunch and dinner selections, priced from $10 to $20, include pasta, beef, veal, fish, seafood, and pork. Also a good choice for Italian food, with entrées priced between $10 and $20, is the oak-paneled dining room of the **Rosebud Cafe**, 1500 W. Taylor, (312) 942-1117. Great warm bread starts the meal, and recommendations include light fried zucchini, escarole soup, and pasta portions large enough for two.

Near the intersection of S. Halsted Street and Jackson, Greek Town has about three blocks of restaurants and coffee shops. The **Parthenon**, 314 S. Halsted, (312) 726-2407, has an extensive, inexpensive menu. The surroundings look a little worn, but the waiters are swift and attentive, and the food is delicious. Try the chicken shish kebabs or juicy gyros, and, for the show, try the flaming saganaki appetizer. Another Greek Town choice is **Rodity's**, 222 S. Halsted, (312) 454-0800, a family-style, bustling place that serves tasty and generous dishes at reasonable prices.

For Mexican food lovers, **Lindo Mexico**, 2642 N. Lincoln Avenue, (312) 871-4832, is one of Chicago's best bargains. (Lincoln runs diagonally from the zoo at Lincoln Park.) An extensive menu offers lavish portions of everything from fajitas to flautas and beef, chicken, and seafood entrées.

**Entertainment**
*The Reader,* a free weekly paper published each Friday, lists all the concert, theater, movie, and special event information you could possibly need. Especially check *The Reader* when summer outdoor festival fever in Chicago and its suburbs generates more than 300 outdoor extravaganzas (many of them free). In June, look for the **Chicago Blues Festival**; from the end of June to the end of August, America's largest free symphonic music festival; the **Taste of Chicago** in Grant Park for one week starting on the Fourth of July; and the grand finale of Grant Park's free summer music festival, the **Chicago Jazz Festival**, Labor Day weekend.

If you can take the crowds, especially on weekends, at **B.L.U.E.S.**, 2519 N. Halstead, (312) 528-1012, and **Kingston Mines** across the street, 2548 N. Halstead, (312) 477-4646, you'll hear the genuine stuff until 4:00 a.m. on Friday and 5:00 a.m. on Saturday for $2 to $7 cover. Less crowded, more civil and pleasant surroundings for local blues talent are found at **Blue Chicago**, 937 N. State, in the Loop, cover $4 to $6, (312) 642-6261; **Lilly's**, 2513 N. Lincoln, (312) 525-2422, and the **Wise Fools Pub**, 2270 N. Lincoln, (312) 929-1510, both in Lincoln Park; and **B.L.U.E.S. ETCETERA**, 1124 W. Belmont, a couple of blocks west of Sheffield, (312) 525-8989. Without going out of your way, you also can hear some excellent jazz nightly at **The Jazz Bulls**, 1916 N. Lincoln Park West, (312) 337-3000.

The **Second City** comedy theater opened its doors at 1616 N. Wells, (312) 337-3992, in 1959 and has been making irreverent waves ever since, producing famous graduates like Bill Murray and John Belushi. A bar stretches along the second level, and cabaret-style tables fill the first floor. Alcoholic and nonalcoholic drinks served without a minimum obviously are a secondary reason for comedy customers who pay a cover of $8.50 on Sunday, Tuesday through Thursday, and $9.50 Saturday.

Stand-up comedy at **Zanies Comedy Nite Club**, 1548 N. Wells, (312) 337-4027, has coexisted with its neighbor club since 1978. The cover is $10 with a two-drink minimum, shows Tuesday through Thursday 8:30 p.m., Friday and Saturday 7:00, 9:00, and 11:15 p.m. The **Funny Firm**, 319 W. Grand, (312) 321-9500, came along in 1987 in a nondescript facility offering stand-up shows Tuesday and Wednesday at 8:30 p.m., Thursday at 7:30 and 9:45 p.m., Friday at 8:00 and 10:30 p.m., Saturday at 7:00, 9:30, and 11:45 p.m., and Sunday at 8:30 p.m. Cover $10 to $12, two-drink minimum. Other comedy clubs like **Catch a Rising Star** at the Hyatt Regency, (312) 565-4242, and **The Improv** at 504 N. Wells, (312) 527-2500, follow similar formats with local and out-of-town talent.

# CHICAGO

Trace the history of the universe in one of the world's great natural history museums and explore the cultures of Egypt, China, and other nations. See the oldest—and one of the most innovative—zoos in the nation. Just down the street, visit Chicago's oldest cultural institution, with fascinating exhibits on the city's past, present, and future. End the day in the festive spirit of Chicago's special summer events with an evening of Chicago-style humor.

## Suggested Itinerary

| | |
|---|---|
| 7:30 a.m. | Breakfast. |
| 9:00 a.m. | Arrive at the Field Museum. |
| 12:30 p.m. | Lunch in the Loop or at the Art Institute. |
| 2:00 p.m. | Visit Lincoln Park and Zoo. |
| 3:30 p.m. | Tour the Chicago Historical Museum. |
| 6:00 p.m. | Dinner in an ethnic restaurant. |
| 8:00 p.m. | Comedy club or other evening entertainment. |

## Sightseeing Highlights

▲▲▲ **The Field Museum of Natural History**—Just across Lake Shore Drive from the Shedd Aquarium, the Field Museum, (312) 922-9410, contains more than nine acres of exhibits—towering dinosaurs, ancient Egyptian mummies, American Indian life, and the rest of life on Earth from prehistoric times to the present day. Open daily 9:00 a.m. to 5:00 p.m. Admission is $2 for adults, $1 for children and students; Thursdays, no admission is charged.

▲▲ **Lincoln Park**—Starting three miles north of Grant Park along the lakeshore, where you can walk all the way, Lincoln Park extends from North Avenue 10 miles north to Hollywood Avenue. With swimming beaches at several points, a boating lagoon near the zoo, boat marinas, and picnic areas everywhere, the park comfortably accommodates thousands of frolicking families without crowding. Located on the park grounds, Theater on the Lake, Fullerton and Lake Shore Drive, (312) 348-7075, presents plays at 8:30 p.m. Tuesday through Saturday, June through August. Tickets are only $1.50.

▲▲ **Lincoln Park Zoological Gardens**—The nation's oldest zoo, Lincoln Park, 2200 N. Cannon Drive, (312) 294-4660, houses on 35 acres more than 2,000 animals, including many exotic and endangered species and one of the largest gorilla collections in the world. A "koala condo" houses three koalas. The zoo is open daily from 9:00 a.m. to 5:00 p.m. Free admission.

▲ **Lincoln Park Conservatory**—Just north of the zoo, stroll in the conservatory's palm house, fern house, and cactus room from 9:00 a.m. to 5:00 p.m. daily, (312) 294-4770. Admission free.

▲▲ **Chicago Historical Society**—At the south end of Lincoln Park, at Clark and North Avenue, (312) 642-4844, the oldest museum and library in the city contains dioramas and galleries devoted to Chicago history. Open Monday through Saturday from 9:30 a.m. to 4:30 p.m. and Sunday from noon to 5:00 p.m. Admission is $1.50 for adults and 50 cents for children 6 to 17. Free admission on Mondays.

▲▲ **The Art Institute of Chicago**—One of the world's best collections of ninteenth- and twentieth-century French art can be seen at the world-famous Art Institute, S. Michigan at Adams, (312) 443-3500. Open Monday through Friday from 10:30 a.m. to 4:30 p.m., Saturdays from 10:00 a.m. to 5:00 p.m., and Sundays and holidays from noon to 5:00 p.m. Admission is $5 for adults and $2.50 for children, students, and senior citizens. Free admission on Tuesdays.

▲▲ **Lake Michigan cruises**—In late spring, summer, and early fall, plan to see Chicago from the lake on one of the daily cruises through the locks and down the Chicago River. Mercury Cruise Lines boards passengers at the lower level of the Michigan Avenue Bridge at Wacker Drive, (312) 332-1368. From April through September,

narrated tours of one to two hours depart at 10:00 a.m.,
11:30 a.m., 3:15 p.m., and 7:30 p.m. The Wendella Sightseeing Boats board at the northwest corner of Michigan
Avenue and the bridge at Wacker Drive, (312) 337-1446.
Tours operate from April through September, departing
daily (weather permitting) at 10:00 a.m., 11:30 a.m., 1:15
p.m., 3:00 p.m., and 7:30 p.m. A narrated tour takes passengers through the locks that separate Lake Michigan
from the Chicago River. Every Wednesday evening, Wendella offers a one-hour cocktail cruise with hors
d'oeuvres.

   Spirit of Chicago, (312) 644-5914, offers a different lake
touring experience—brunch, lunch, or dinner, two
bands and a show, moonlight party cruises, "Tropical
Thursday Party Cruises," or just sightseeing. Tours depart
from the south side of the Navy Pier at Grand Avenue,
and tickets are $24 to $49. Likewise, check out lake tours
by Stars of Chicago, also docked at the Navy Pier.

# MILWAUKEE AND MADISON

See, taste, and smell the influences of German heritage in Milwaukee. After a sampling of cultural and culinary arts along the city's lake- and riverfronts, drive past wooded hills and farmlands, barns and silos to Madison. Along the way, spend as much of the afternoon as possible at fascinating Old World Wisconsin. In Madison, enjoy a memorable evening of relaxation along the University of Wisconsin's lakeshore.

## Suggested Schedule

| | |
|---|---|
| 8:00 a.m. | Breakfast and leave Chicago for Milwaukee. |
| 10:30 a.m. | View the lake from the Milwaukee Art Museum. |
| 11:30 a.m. | Visit the Grand Avenue Mall. |
| 12:00 noon | Lunch on Old World Third Street or in the Mall. |
| 1:00 p.m. | Leave for Old World Wisconsin. |
| 5:00 p.m. | Leave Old World Wisconsin for Madison. |
| 6:30 p.m. | Check into Madison lodgings. |
| 7:30 p.m. | Dinner in downtown Madison. |
| 9:30 p.m. | Stroll along Lake Mendota at the university. |

**Travel Route: Chicago to Milwaukee (94 miles)**
Take I-90/94 (Edens Expressway) north out of Chicago. It's 57 miles to Kenosha and 37 miles from there to Milwaukee. Drive directly to Milwaukee unless you have time for a detour through Kenosha and Racine. Take Highway 158 east (52nd Street) from I-94 in Kenosha to Sheridan Road south to 60th Street to see the preserved mansions in the Third Avenue Historic District. From Kenosha, take Highway 32 north to Lighthouse Drive on Racine's north side to the Windpoint Lighthouse, the tallest (112 feet) and oldest lighthouse on the Great Lakes. Inside, 144 steps lead to a great view from the top. Return on 4 Mile Road west to I-94. In spring, stop at Milaeger's. Take a left

on Douglas to 4838 Douglas Avenue, (414) 639-2040, to
see their 57 greenhouses with over 700 varieties of perennials and more than 200 kinds of bedding plants.

In Milwaukee, take I-94 to I-794 east and exit at Lincoln
Memorial Drive north along the lakefront to the War
Memorial and Milwaukee Art Museum on your right,
below Juneau Park. From the museum, take Mason to the
corner of N. Milwaukee and E. Mason to pick up maps,
brochures, and listings of current events at the Greater
Milwaukee Convention and Visitors Bureau, (414)
273-7222. From there, turn left on the next street, Broadway, and take the first right on Wisconsin. Follow Wisconsin across the Milwaukee River to the Grand Avenue
Mall. From there you can walk down Old World Third
Street for sightseeing and lunch, without moving your
vehicle. Without receipts, parking in the mall costs $1.50
for three hours; buy anything and it's free for three hours.

If you want to skip the lakefront stop, take I-94 to I-794
east, exit at Plankinton and drive straight ahead to the
mall's parking structure.

## Milwaukee
An international seaport, Milwaukee still retains the feel-
ing and attitudes of a small town. A collection of tidy
neighborhoods that can boast of 137 parks, this conser-
vative factory town is working hard to become a cos-
mopolitan city, with core values affirming quality of life.
The airport is outstanding in design and efficiency, the
zoo is great, and any city would be proud of its art and
natural history museums. Even the downtown's modern
high-rise buildings are interspersed with enough restored
nineteenth-century buildings to keep old and new in bal-
ance. With one of the few urban skywalk systems connecting hotels, theaters, restaurants, and other buildings
in the new Milwaukee Center and the downtown, chill,
off-season weather shouldn't keep you from visiting.

The Milwaukee River divides the downtown into east
and west sections before it enters Lake Michigan. From
the Milwaukee River, streets are numbered in ascending

order westward into the suburbs. Wisconsin Avenue is the main east-west thoroughfare. The central business district is only a few blocks wide. The east, west, and south sides of the river each have historic neighborhoods and excellent restaurants. Several botanical gardens in the region are as pretty as you'll see anywhere in the United States.

Milwaukee's major wholesaling and manufacturing district, the Third Ward, was gutted by a fire in 1892 that destroyed 440 buildings. Rebuilt with a handsome variety of architectural styles in 1984, the ten-square-block area of the Third Ward obtained designation from the National Register of Historic Places as "The Historic Third Ward District." An architectural and historical walking tour of about 32 buildings takes about an hour and a half comfortably. For information on other short walking tours in the historic districts of Kilbourntown, Walker's Point, or the east side mansion area, contact Historic Milwaukee, Inc., ArchiTours, (414) 277-7795.

**Sightseeing Highlights**
▲▲ **The Milwaukee Art Museum**—Located in the lakefront War Memorial Center, the museum, 750 North Lincoln Memorial Drive, (414) 271-9508, offers a strong permanent collection of nineteenth- and twentieth-century European and American art (Degas, Toulouse-Lautrec, Miró, Picasso, O'Keeffe, Warhol, etc.) and excellent special exhibits. View Milwaukee's scenic lakefront there on a nice day. Open Tuesday, Wednesday, Friday, and Saturday from 10:00 a.m. to 5:00 p.m., Thursday from noon to 9:00 p.m., and Sunday from noon to 5:00 p.m. Admission is $3 for adults, $1.50 for students and seniors over 59; free to children 12 and under accompanied by an adult.
▲▲ **The Grand Avenue Mall**—Four city blocks and five historic buildings connected by glass skywalks create multilevel shopping from Marshall Field's on the west side of the river to the Boston Store on Wisconsin. This is

a good place to have an inexpensive lunch, especially for
those who love choices—a wide selection of ethnic
food, health food, and traditional fare and desserts. Try
the mesquite-smoked meats and fresh rolls and corn-
bread at Apricot Annie's on the street level arcade off 2nd
Street.

▲ **Renaissance Book Shop**—At 834 N. Plankinton Ave,
down the street from the mall, (414) 271-6850, this is a
wonderful place for lovers of old books—five floors of
books in a dilapidated building that looks and feels more
like Haight-Ashbury or SoHo than Milwaukee. (Somehow
the owners have managed to transfer some of this atmosphere and thousands of used books to an outpost concession at the Milwaukee Airport.)

▲ **Milwaukee Center**—Across the river, Milwaukee's
new Performing Arts Center, 139 E. Kilbourn Avenue,
(414) 276-8686, and the Wyndham Hotel and offices feature an interesting interior design combination of marble,
mahogany, and corrugated metal.

▲▲ **The Old World Third Street Area**—For another
glimpse of old Milwaukee, cross the river again on E. State
to Pere Marquette Park and briefly visit the Milwaukee
County Historical Center, 910 Old World Street. Open
weekdays 9:30 a.m. to 5:00 p.m., Saturday 10:00 a.m. to
5:00 p.m., and Sunday 1:00 to 5:00 p.m.; admission free.
The nearby red brick paved streets of Old World Third
Street lead you to historic architecture and Old World-
quality delectables. In the heart of this old German business district, landmarks include Unsinger's Famous
Sausage (when was the last time you had Unsinger's
Braunschweiger liver sausage and thinly sliced Bermuda
onion on rye?) and the Wisconsin Cheese Mart, 215 W.
Highland Avenue.

▲ **The Pabst Brewery Tours**—A 40-minute free tour
on the hour from June through August, weekdays 10:00
a.m. to 3:00 p.m., Saturday 9:00 a.m. to 11:00 p.m., tells
you a great deal about brewing and its part in the history
of Milwaukee. Take N. 6th to W. Juneau, then turn left on
W. Juneau to the brewery, 915 W. Juneau.

▲ **The Milwaukee Public Museum**—One of the nation's foremost natural history museums has fascinating and surprising exhibits, like the show of 250 live species of Wisconsin wildflowers, which was scheduled simultaneously with more than 70 paintings celebrating the 200th anniversary of *Curtis's Botanical Magazine*, one of the world's oldest and most respected horticulture magazines. Exhibit Hall hours are Monday noon to 8:00 p.m., Tuesday to Sunday 9:00 a.m. to 5:00 p.m. Admission is $4 for adults, $2 for children 4 to 17. Located at 800 W. Wells Street, which is one-way east, adjacent to I-43 and 7th, (414) 278-2702.

▲ **The Pabst Mansion**—A few miles west of the river at 2000 W. Wisconsin, the mansion was built in 1893 for beer baron Captain Frederick Pabst. The mansion has 37 rooms, 12 baths, and 14 fireplaces. Tours take about 90 minutes. Admission is $4 for adults, $2.50 for children 6 to 16, children under 6 free. Hours: March 15 to December 31, Monday through Saturday 10:00 a.m. to 3:30 p.m., Sunday noon to 3:30 p.m.; and January 1 to March 14, Saturday 10:00 a.m. to 3:30 p.m., Sunday noon to 3:30 p.m.

▲ **Mitchell Park Horticultural Conservatory**—The Domes, 524 South Layton Boulevard, (414) 649-9800, was built to exhibit plant collections from tropical as well as arid regions of the world. The beehive-shaped Show Dome (floricultural exhibits), Tropical Dome (plants of the tropical rain forests), and Arid Dome each are 140 feet wide and 85 feet high and cover an area of 15,000 square feet. Open daily 9:00 a.m. to 5:00 p.m.; $2.50 for adults, $1 for kids under 18, $1.25 for senior Milwaukee County residents.

**Food**

In Milwaukee, you'll pass **Karl Ratzsch's Old World Restaurant**, 320 E. Mason Street, (414) 276-2620, which serves lunch every day except Monday and dinner every day. Traditional German specialties are as good here as anywhere in Milwaukee. **Mader's German Restaurant**, 1037-41 North Old World Third Street, (414) 271-3377,

more than 80 years old, serves classic German food.
Hours are Monday 11:30 a.m. to 9:00 p.m., Tuesday
through Saturday 11:30 a.m. to 11:30 p.m., Sunday 10:30
a.m. to 9:00 p.m., with a Viennese brunch on Sunday.
Afterward, cure your sweet tooth at the **Ambrosia
Chocolate Co.,** 6th and Highland Avenue, the world's
largest manufacturer of bulk chocolate. On days when
the wind is right, you can follow your nose to the factory
without paying attention to street signs.

Historic Walker's Point, listed in the National Register
of Historic Places, south of where the Menomenee River
flows into the Milwaukee River, has a high percentage of
turn-of-the-century buildings. Between 1st and 2nd
streets are ten of Milwaukee's most enjoyable pubs with
quaint names like Chumps Rusty Bucket and Louis's
Ancient Chinese Tavern. On the west side of Walker's
Point are two restaurants that will show you another facet
of Milwaukee. **Chip & Py's**, 815 S. 5th, (414) 645-3435,
closed Mondays, is open from 5:00 p.m. until after
11:00 p.m. (live jazz on weekends from 8:00 to midnight).
**Mike & Anna's Restaurant**, 1978 S. 8th Street, (414)
643-0072, from the outside looks like a neighborhood
tavern but is one of Milwaukee's finest intimate, expensive, gourmet restaurants. The dining room is small (only
12 tables), and decor is sparse but elegant. Reservations
are required on summer weekends. The kitchen is open
from 5:30 to 9:00 p.m. Closed Mondays.

**Travel Route: Milwaukee to Madison via Old World
Wisconsin (90 miles)**
Take I-94 west toward Madison to the Highway 67 exit at
Delafield, and drive 12 miles south to the village of Eagle
and another mile on Highway 67 to Old World Wiscon-
sin. The drive takes about one hour from Milwaukee to
Old World Wisconsin and another hour from there to
Madison, returning the same way, north to I-94, and then
continuing west on I-94 to Madison. (If you decide to
bypass Milwaukee, take Highway 12 from Chicago to

## Milwaukee-Madison-Wisconsin Dells

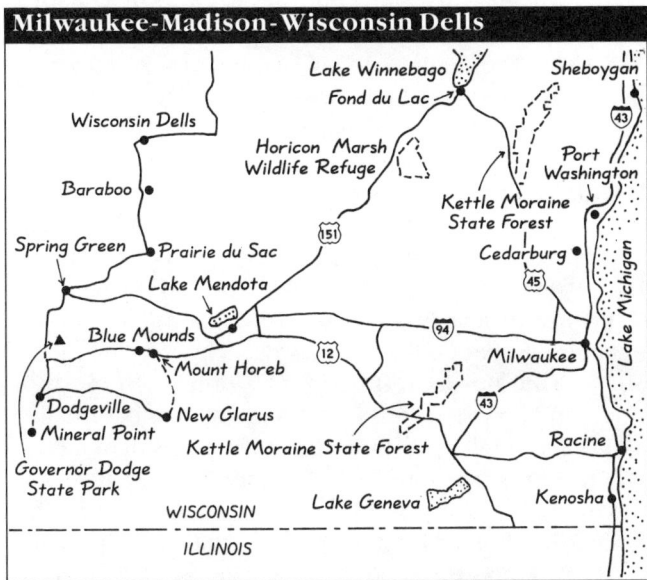

Highway 67 to Eagle and Old World Wisconsin.) The
shortest, if not the prettiest, way into Madison from I-94
is to exit on route 30 to E. Washington Avenue and turn
left toward the State Capitol.

### Sightseeing Highlights

▲▲▲ **Old World Wisconsin**—Nestled on a 576-acre
site in the rolling hills of beautiful **Kettle Moraine State
Forest**, Old World Wisconsin, Highway 67, Eagle, (414)
594-2116, is a living museum. Accenting the life-styles of
different ethnic groups, fifty structures actually built by
Wisconsin's pioneers in the nineteenth and early twentieth centuries have been relocated into a crossroads village complex operated by authentically costumed staff
who perform daily chores and seasonal activities just as
they were done more than 100 years ago. See German,
Norwegian, Danish, and Finnish farmsteads. The exhibits
cover 2½ miles and a minimum of 4 hours to view.
Throughout the year, special events are tied to the sea-

sons, like threshing time, a midsummer festival, and holidays. Open daily from May 1 through October 31, 10:00
a.m. to 5:00 p.m. Admission is $6 for adults, $4.80 for
people over 65, $2.50 for children under 15, and $10 for
families.

**Lodging**
In Madison, drive down Wisconsin Street from the State
Capitol to the end, where you will see the **Edgewater
Hotel**, (800) 922-5512, overlooking Lake Mendota. It is
somewhat expensive at $75 to $85 singles and doubles
but a good value. Or drive down fraternity row on Langdon
Street to the **Madison Inn**, 601 Langdon, (608) 257-4391,
single and double queen $53 to $58. (Remember the
additional 12% tax in Wisconsin.) The inn is right next to
downtown and the university campus. It's a short walk to
the Union Theater at 800 Langdon and about a half mile
to the Civic Center, in the Capitol and historical museum
area. The **University Inn** just off State, 441 N. Francis,
(608) 257-4881, is closer to the Civic Center and the Capitol area and about the same price and quality as the Madison Inn.

   Madison also has a variety of appealing B&Bs like
**Annie's**, 2117 Sheridan Drive, (608) 244-2224, one block
from Lake Mendota. This cedar shake and stucco house
overlooks a beautiful valley and Warner Park and offers
three guest rooms, with wood-burning stove and hot tub,
at $65 to $85. The lovely **Lakehouse**, 4027 Monona
Drive, (800) 397-8261, has great views to the lake, canoes
and bikes for your use, and the Caroline Suite for honey-
mooners and other lovers. Room costs range from $25 to
$90. The recently renovated Greek Revival **Plough Inn**,
3402 Monroe Street, (608) 238-2901, overlooks Lake
Wingra and the UW Arboretum, a marvelous hiking and
cross-country skiing area. Rooms cost $55 to $89,
depending on the season, day of the week, and room.

## Camping

**Lake Kegonsa State Park**, 5 miles northwest of Stough-
ton and 12 miles southeast of Madison off U.S. 51 on
Door Creek Road, has 80 wooded campsites without
showers and electricity for $6 a night, (608) 873-9695.
Reservations accepted for groups only. There's a very nice
beach on this 3,200-acre "Lake of the Many Fishes,"
which does have good fishing, and more than 60 acres of
reestablished prairie with nature trails. From I-94, take
I-90 south to the County Highway N exit, turn right in
about 5 miles on County Highway B where you'll come
to the access road to Lake Kegonsa.

Your best bet in Madison is a private campground.
**KOA Madison**, 4859 County Highway V, DeForest, WI
53532, (608) 846-4528, has 81 sites with showers at $12 a
night, $2.50 additional for electricity. From the junction
of I-90 and I-94, drive 6 miles north on I-90/94 to exit
126, County Highway V and the campground. It's easy to
get back into the city on Highway 51 south to E. Washington Street or on County Highway V to Highway 113.

## Food

**Kabul Restaurant**, 541 State Street, just steps from the
Madison Inn, serves superb Afghan cuisine that sounds
and is exotic but will delight adventuresome travelers.
The Zafari brothers have concocted some of the tastiest
meals in town for around $10 with appetizers. I suggest
that you start with mashawa, an Afghan-style soup made
with a variety of beans, chicken, beef, lamb, rice, cilantro,
and dill. Then have mahi, a fresh fillet of catfish sauteed
with fresh mushrooms and scallions and served in a rich
sauce of tomatoes, tumeric, pepper, cilantro, and parsley.
Kabul is open from 11:00 a.m. to 10:30 p.m. seven days a
week.

The **Espresso Royale Cafe**, 650 State Street, serves on
the sidewalk or indoors Monday through Saturday from
7:00 a.m. to midnight. The menu includes cafe latte,
other coffees, teas, hot and cold drinks, and pastries.

**Sunprint Cafe & Gallery**, upstairs at 638 State Street, is
excellent for light dishes. Open daily until 10:00 p.m.

**Itinerary Option**
**In Milwaukee, Boerner's Botanical Garden** is a
marvelous showcase of native trees and shrubs. This
1,000-acre arboretum is in **Whitnall Park**, adjoining the
Root River Parkway. The park also has about 1,000
crabapple trees, including about 250 species and varieties. The *Milwaukee Journal*-sponsored **Rose Festival**
at the gardens in the third week of June is a must for rose
lovers from anywhere. The gardens are an out-of-the-
way option, requiring at least a half-day's trip to the far
southwest corner of the Milwaukee metropolitan area.
From I-894 take the W. Forest Home exit (24), along
W. Forest Home past the Root River Parkway to S. 92nd
Street, and then to the gardens' entrance.

# MADISON, MT. HOREB, LITTLE NORWAY, AND CAVE OF THE MOUNDS

Visit one of the state's best art museums, tour the Wisconsin State Capitol, and sample the state's culture and history at the State Historical Society Museum in central Madison. Enjoy a walk and picnic lunch in one of the Midwest's loveliest gardens before heading west to Mt. Horeb, Spring Green, and across the Wisconsin River. Along the way, see a museum of regional folk history, sample some of Wisconsin's best cheese, and visit Little Norway. Tour a remarkable cave at Blue Mounds, and then drive from Spring Green through one of Wisconsin's scenic valleys to the foot of the rocky Baraboo Range and Devil's Lake State Park.

## Suggested Schedule

| | |
|---|---|
| 8:00 a.m. | Breakfast in Madison. |
| 8:45 a.m. | Stroll on the university campus to the Elvehjem Museum of Art. |
| 9:00 a.m. | Tour the Elvehjem Museum of Art. |
| 10:30 a.m. | Tour the State Capitol. |
| 11:30 a.m. | Visit the State Historical Society Museum. |
| 12:30 p.m. | Picnic lunch at Olbrich Gardens. |
| 1:30 p.m. | Leave for Mt. Horeb. |
| 2:00 p.m. | See the Wisconsin Folk Museum in Mt. Horeb. |
| 2:45 p.m. | Visit Little Norway. |
| 3:45 p.m. | Tour Cave of the Mounds. |
| 5:15 p.m. | Drive on WI Highway 60 toward Baraboo. |
| 6:30 p.m. | Check-in and dinner in the Devil's Lake/Baraboo area. |

## Madison

Known as the Four Lakes (Mendota, Monona, Wingra, and Waubesa) when it was made the territorial capital in 1837, Madison was built out of wilderness on a narrow strip of land separating Lakes Mendota and Monona.

On one hill, the Capitol was built; on another to the west,
the University of Wisconsin along the shoreline of Lake
Mendota. The city contains 18,000 acres of lakes, 150
parks with 3,500 acres of recreation area, and more than
25 performing arts theaters and museums. The architectural history of the city is enriched with many of Frank
Lloyd Wright's buildings. The city is dominated by the
university, by State Street, the main commercial
thoroughfare, and by Lake Mendota.

**Sightseeing Highlights**
▲ **State Street**—Good weather brings everyone out to
sidewalk cafes and restaurant gathering spots on State
Street, the university's "Main Street," which runs from
Lake Mendota and the campus to the State Capitol.
▲ **Wisconsin Union Theater**—The theater opens onto
Lake Mendota and has tables and chairs on a lakeside
patio where you can wait for performances to begin or
just have a snack and enjoy the lake. The Union Theater
brings distinguished national and international concert
and performing arts groups to Madison. Local demand
for seats is always strong, and reservations are essential.
(608) 262-2201.
▲ **The Madison Civic Center**—About a half mile up
State Street from the Union Theater, the Civic Center is a
first-rate place to find music, theater, dance, or other
entertainment. Ballet Français de Nancy, the New York
City Opera National Company, P.D.Q. Bach, Broadway
shows, and the Modern Jazz Quartet are just some of the
many fine events. Call 24 hours (608) 656-2728.
▲▲ **Elvehjem Museum of Art**—One of the outstanding small museums (more than 13,500 works of art) of the
Midwest in terms of design and exhibition content, the
museum, 800 University Avenue, (608) 263-2246, includes Egyptian art, Near Eastern artifacts, ancient Greek
ceramics, medieval, Renaissance, and baroque art, four
collections of Asian and Oriental art, Japanese prints, Rus-
sian icons and paintings, and American and European art
of the last three centuries. Open Monday through Satur-

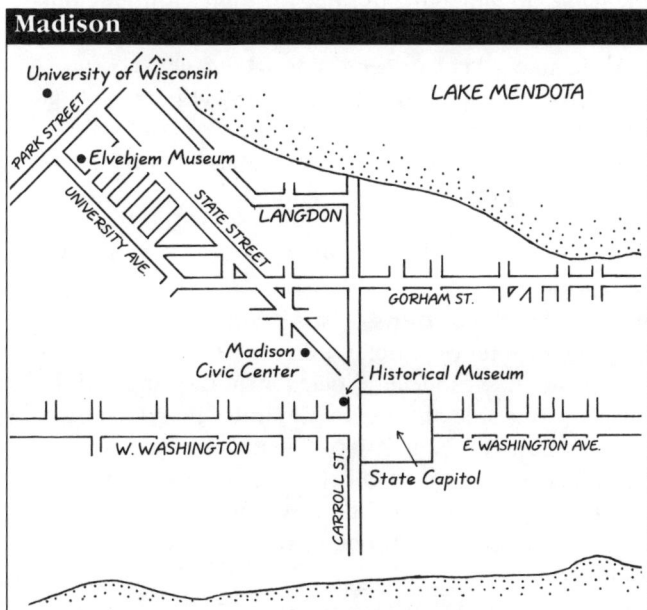

**Madison**

University of Wisconsin

PARK STREET

Elvehjem Museum

UNIVERSITY AVE.

STATE STREET

LANGDON

LAKE MENDOTA

GORHAM ST.

Madison
Civic Center

Historical Museum

W. WASHINGTON

CARROLL ST.

E. WASHINGTON AVE.

State Capitol

day from 9:00 a.m. to 4:45 p.m., Sunday from 11:00 a.m. to 4:45 p.m. Admission free.

▲▲ **Wisconsin State Capitol**—Free tours of this impressive Roman Renaissance structure's rotunda, legislative chambers, Supreme Court, and governor's conference room operate daily from 9:00 to 11:00 a.m. and 1:00 to 4:00 p.m., starting at the information desk in the rotunda, (608) 266-0382.

▲▲ **State Historical Society Museum and Gift Shop**—This museum at 30 N. Carroll Street, just across the street from the State Capitol at the southeast corner of the State Capitol square, covers prehistoric times to the present. The gift shop is beautifully designed, lighted, and staffed with helpful people. The shop has all the books on Wisconsin that one could possibly want to browse through or buy, including travel literature. Ask for a *Book & Gift Catalogue* to take with you. Hours are

10:00 a.m. to 5:00 p.m. Tuesday through Saturday, Sunday noon to 5:00 p.m. Admission free.

▲▲ **Madison Art Center**—This facility at 211 State Street, the Civic Center, (608) 256-0029, operates six gallery areas on four floors, showing the work of local, regional, and national artists. There's also a good gift shop. Open Tuesday through Thursday 11:00 a.m. to 5:00 p.m., Friday 11:00 a.m. to 9:00 p.m., Saturday 10:00 a.m. to 5 p.m., and Sunday 1:00 p.m. to 5:00 p.m. Admission free.

▲▲▲ **Olbrich Gardens**—This beautiful facility includes 15 acres of annuals, perennials, shrubs, hybrid roses, and lilies, especially spectacular in spring. On the Lake Monona side of the State Capitol, take Williamson Street to Eastwood and Atwood Avenue, which bends around Lake Monona to Olbrich Gardens, 3330 Atwood Avenue, (608) 246-4551. Open daily April through September and Monday through Friday the rest of the year. Admission free.

**Travel Route: Madison to Devil's Lake (57 miles)**
From Madison, take Highways 18/151 west to Mt. Horeb, continue on Highway 18 to Highway JG North, and then follow signs to Cave of the Mounds Road. Continue through Blue Mounds and Dodgeville, then turn north on Highway 23/14 to Spring Green across the Wisconsin River. Turn northeast on scenic Highway 60 and see beautiful Jones Valley along the Wisconsin River, turning north on WI 12. Turn right on WI 59 to County Highway DL, and turn right again to the entrance to Devil's Lake State Park. If instead of turning right on County Highway DL you turn left on Highway 123 to Baraboo, you'll find the accommodations suggested below for noncampers.

**Sightseeing Highlights**
▲▲ **Wisconsin Folk Art Museum**—This small museum, 100 S. 2nd Street, Mt. Horeb, (608) 437-4742, has unusual regional displays: the largest collection of

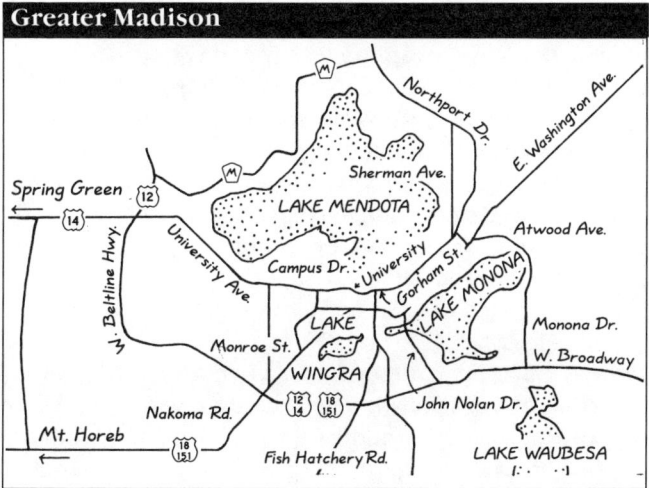

**Greater Madison**

wood sculptures by north woods artist Jerry Holter,
including life-sized carvings of Indians and soaring
eagles; Norwegian-American rosemaling, a colorful floral
folk art on bowls, tankards, and cupboards; and a beautiful collection of painted Ukrainian eggs by Betty Pisia
Christenson. The museum gift shop offers books and
musical recordings, such as Swiss folk music and
Norwegian-American and German-American old-time
music recordings from Wisconsin that are some of the
best produced in America. The museum's director, folk-
lorist Philip Martin, has written and published the defini-
tive book, *Rosemaling in the Upper Midwest*, which contains 70 full-color photographs.
▲ **Ryser Cheese Factory**—Across the street from the
folk art museum, peek through the window of this
award-winning cheese factory to see vats of cheese in
production. Pick up some cheese and sausage in the gift
shop. The best Muenster cheese in the United States is
said to come from Mt. Horeb. No other cheese factory in
Wisconsin produces a greater variety of cheeses. Try their
Palatelle and creamy dill cheeses.

▲ **Antiques**—More people come to Mt. Horeb to buy antiques than cheese. See why on four floors of the **Mt. Horeb Trading Company**, 132 E. Main Street, (608) 437-5071, for refinished antiques, and **Yapp's Antique Corner**, Springdale and Main, (608) 437-8100, with 25 dealers on three floors, and others.

▲▲ **Little Norway**—See a collection of Norse antiques and items used by Scandinavian pioneers in a homestead within a pretty wooded valley among the foothills of the Blue Mounds. From Highway 18, take a right on County Highway E, a left on County Highway ID, then a right on County Highway JG to Little Norway, (608) 437-8211. The Norway Building, patterned after a twelfth-century Stavkirke, a Christian Norwegian church, was built in Norway for exhibition at the Chicago World's Columbian Exposition in 1893. Open 9:00 a.m. to 5:00 p.m. May and June and September and October, and 9:00 a.m. to 7:00 p.m. July and August. Admission is $4.50 for adults and $2 for children 6 to 12.

▲▲ **Cave of the Mounds**—A National Historic Landmark, the caves have very unusual stalagmites, stalactites, and pools discovered by the owner of a historic farm who was quarrying for limestone. The cave tour takes about an hour and begins every 15 minutes after a video preview. The grounds have pleasant picnic sites. Bring a sweater or jacket, since the caves are at a constant 50 degrees F. From Little Norway, return to County ID, turn right and then right again on Cave of the Mounds Road in Blue Mounds. The phone number is (608) 437-3038. The caves are 3 miles west of Mt. Horeb and just 20 miles west of Madison. Open every day, 9:00 a.m. to 7:00 p.m. Admission $6.50 adults, $3 children 5 to 12.

▲ **Taliesin/Hillside Home School**—Built by Frank Lloyd Wright in 1911 as his summer home on a hillside overlooking the Wisconsin River, Taliesin, (608) 588-2511, is a few miles south of Spring Green on Highway 23. Formerly a progressive school operated in the 1880s by Wright's aunts, Hillside became summer headquarters of the Wright Foundation, which continues the architectural firm and school started by Wright. Reflecting Wright's philosophy that a building should grow out of its natural surroundings, Taliesin's eaves of sandstone and oak extend low to the ground over a walled garden. A guided tour of the theater and dining and living spaces leaves daily on the hour, from 9:00 a.m. until 4:00 p.m. Admission $5 adults, $2 children under 12. At 1:30 p.m. Wednesday through Friday and 2:30 p.m. Saturday, June through September, the foundation offers a worthwhile 1½ hour walking tour of Taliesin beginning at the Hillside Home School, continuing past the Romeo and Juliet Windmill, Tanyderi, Midway Farm, and through the gardens, for $10.50 adults and $4.20 children.

▲ **Tower Hill State Park**—Across the road from Taliesin and across the river from Spring Green, Tower Hill contains the remains of the vanished village of Helena, which produced lead shot in the mid-nineteenth century from lead mined in the area. One of only a handful of shot towers left in the world, the restored 60-foot shaft built next to the cliff extends 120 feet below ground, 180 feet from smelter to collector basin. The view from the shot tower over the Wisconsin River is marvelous.

**Lodging**

**The Farm Kitchen's** cottages on Highway 123 between Devil's Lake and Baraboo are priced under $35 for two, (608) 365-5246. The Kuesters (see Food, below) also own **The Barn Motel**, (608) 356-5511, a few hundred feet down the road, with clean, air-conditioned rooms at $25 for two. **Grandpa's Gate**, (608) 493-2755, a B&B and country store in Baraboo, is reached from Highway 123 to Lower DL, then turn left. The rates are $40 single and $50 double. Ask about nearby Parfrey Glenn and Durwood Glenn, two beautiful areas for walking. In the town of Baraboo itself is the **House of Seven Gables B&B**, 215 6th Street, (608) 356-8387, a Gothic/Victorian gingerbread house on the National Register of Historic Places. Elegant rooms are furnished entirely with pieces dating from 1860 to 1880. Pam and Ralph Krainik provide delicious, very full breakfasts. Rooms are $53 single and $60 double. The gardens are lovely, too.

## Camping
**Devil's Lake State Park**, S5975 Park Road, Baraboo, WI 53913, (608) 356-8301, three miles south of Baraboo off Highway 123, has 459 campsites, including Ice Age, 206 sites without electricity; Northern Lights, 121 sites with electricity; and Quartzite, 100 sites with electricity. All of these campgrounds have showers. Reservations are essential between June 15 and Labor Day. (See Sightseeing Highlights, Day 5.)

## Food
**Schubert's** on Main Street in Mt. Horeb has been serving three home-cooked meals a day to demanding customers since 1911. The Swedish rye, other bakery items, and food are excellent and reasonable. Open daily 7:30 a.m. to 9:00 p.m.

Tom and Darla Kuester's **The Farm Kitchen** on Highway 123 is one of the friendliest, most hospitable places in Wisconsin, which is saying a lot. They serve a delicious assortment of chicken, meat, and fish dishes, with a big, excellent salad bar, at prices that exceed $10 only for 16 oz. boneless top sirloin and porterhouse steaks and huge seafood platters. Homemade desserts are superb. Open daily 7:00 a.m. to 9:00 p.m. Try their deluxe smorgasbord on Sunday from noon to 4:00 p.m.

# BARABOO AND WISCONSIN DELLS

Today you'll see the sculpted grandeur of Devil's Lake and the Wisconsin Dells, 15 miles of rugged and beautiful river scenery. Those spectacular areas were created by glaciers that carved the Wisconsin River's sinuous channel to Milwaukee. Between these two scenic showcases of nature, you'll see the "greatest (man-made) show on earth" live and also in a fascinating museum in historic Baraboo. After lunch, you'll drive to an international sanctuary and breeding and research center for cranes. The day ends with a nighttime boat cruise on the Upper Dells.

## Suggested Schedule

| | |
|---|---|
| 7:30 a.m. | Breakfast. |
| 8:15 a.m. | See Devil's Lake. |
| 10:30 a.m. | Head for Baraboo. |
| 11:00 a.m. | Visit the Al Ringling Theater and explore Baraboo's historic district. |
| 12:00 noon | Lunch. |
| 1:00 p.m. | See the Circus World Museum. |
| 3:30 p.m. | Leave for Wisconsin Dells. |
| 4:00 p.m. | Tour the International Crane Foundation. |
| 5:30 p.m. | Arrive at Wisconsin Dells and check in. |
| 6:30 p.m. | Dinner. |
| 8:45 p.m. | Boat trip to the Stand Rock Indian Ceremonial. |

**Travel Route: Devil's Lake to Wisconsin Dells (7 miles)**

Take Highway 123 to downtown Baraboo and park in the vicinity of the Sauk County Courthouse Square. The square is in the middle of the Downtown Baraboo Historic District. Leave Baraboo on Rt. 33E (Ringling Boulevard) to County Highway A, then left on Shady Lane Road to the International Crane Foundation. Continue north on County Highway A, and take a left on County Highway U to Highway 12 north.

If you're heading for Moon Lake State Park campground near Wisconsin Dells (see Camping, below), stay on scenic County A to Moon Road, then left on Moon Road to the park. After you've checked into the campground, return on Highway 23 to Highway 12 on the other side of I-90/I-94 in Lake Delton. You'll see many of the Dells' attractions clustered along Highway 12 and Highway 23 east into the Wisconsin Dells. If you plan to camp near the Dells at a private campground, continue driving along Highway 12 past the turnoff to Broadway (Highway 23). Several campgrounds near the Dells are suggested below.

## Sightseeing Highlights

▲▲▲ **Devil's Lake**—One of the oldest places in North America, Devil's Lake was created when an Ice Age glacier wrapped around the Baraboo Range, melted, and dumped enough debris to move the old Wisconsin River bed nine miles to the east and create the lake. The Baraboo Bluffs overlooking Devil's Lake, terminal moraines left by the Wisconsin Glacier, offer a beautiful view of 5,100-acre Devil's Lake State Park, its lake, and the Wisconsin River on the horizon. One of the most beautiful and busiest parks in the state, it's always crowded on summer weekends. Come midweek or off-season. Admission to the park, (608) 356-8301, without a sticker is $3.50 for residents, $6 for nonresidents.

▲▲▲ **Circus World Museum/Circus World**— Baraboo is the Ringling Bros. original winter quarters. The "Ringling Classic and Comic Concert Co." of the 1880s became the famous Ringling Bros. and Barnum & Bailey Circus. From the courthouse square, head east on 4th Street to East Street, turn right and drive four blocks to Water Street, then turn left. The circus museum is on your right and parking is on your left past the museum.

Circus World is open May 6 through September 17, with big top shows, demonstrations, concerts, and exhibits. Winter hours at Circus World Museum, 426 Water Street, are Monday to Sunday 9:00 a.m. to 5:00 p.m., Saturday 11:00 a.m. to 5:00 p.m. Admission for adults is

$3.25, children $1.75. The summer season, with the outdoor circus, runs May 5 through September 16, 9:00 a.m.
to 6:00 p.m. Admission for adults is $8.95, children 3 to
12 $5.50, children under 3 free. Showtimes under the big
top are 11:00 a.m. and 3:00 p.m., with starlight shows at
8:00 p.m. July 21 through August 22. Illusionist acts are at
1:00 p.m. and 7:00 p.m.

A combined ticket—"Circus, Cranes and Trains"—to
the Circus World Museum, the International Crane Foundation, and the Mid-Continent Railway Museum (see
Itinerary Options) costs $12.95 for adults and $6.50 for
children. Note: When the circus is outdoors in season,
allow at least a half-day, or more if possible, to see 50
acres of live performances and exhibits.

▲▲▲ **The Al Ringling Theater**—A one-third-scale
model of the Great Opera Hall of the famous Palace of
Versailles near Paris, the theater opened in 1915 across
from the county courthouse. The theater has had a great
history of shows stopping on their way from New York to
Chicago. It was restored in 1978-80. Al Ringling Theatre
Friends, Inc., recently acquired the theater to preserve it
and are still raising money to maintain it. The theater is
the grandest architectural surprise you'll ever have in a
small town. Stop by during daytime hours at 136 Fourth
Avenue, (608) 356-8080, and ask Susan Henkel, manager,
to let you see the theater.

▲▲ **Baraboo's Downtown Historic District**—Stroll
around the Sauk County Courthouse Square and the
Southside Historic District adjoining the Baraboo River
on Ash and Walnut streets. From 4th and Ash, walk down
to the river and across to Walnut. From the Baraboo
Chamber of Commerce Office, 124 Second Avenue, pick
up a copy of *A Guide to Historic Baraboo* and *A
Walking-Historic Tour Guide of Baraboo, Wisconsin*, for
a listing of historic buildings and their locations.

▲▲▲ **International Crane Foundation's Johnson
Exhibit Pod**—Twelve of the world's 15 species of cranes
are bred at the ICF, the most complete collection anywhere, including six endangered species (red-crowned

crane, Siberian crane, whooping crane, hooded crane,
white-naped crane, and wattled crane). Be sure to purchase the ICF's *Field Guide to Crane Behavior* (75 cents)
and the *Guide to the Johnson Exhibit Pod* ($1.05). The
ICF also has a birding trail with more than 20 types of
birds that live in different habitats (grasslands, wetlands,
woodlands, etc.). Hours are 9:00 a.m. to 5:00 p.m. May 1
through October 31. Admission is $3.75 adults, $1.75
children.

▲▲▲ **The Dells**—One of the most spectacular areas
along the Wisconsin River, the Dells is the scenic climax
of four hundred meandering miles of the Wisconsin
River. The Winnebago Indians' lore says that a huge
thrashing serpent heading for the sea carved the craggy
forms. Geologists say that great melting glaciers carved
into Cambrian sandstone to create a new channel for the
Wisconsin River and the seven-mile rocky gorge known
as the Dells (an Americanization of the French name
*Dalles* for the layers of rock that resemble flagstones).
Cliffs rise a hundred feet above the water. A dam divides
the area into Upper and Lower Dells. Most of the scenic
grandeur is in the Upper Dells.

A tourist mecca for more than 70 years, starting with
Indian powwows organized as a nightly event in the
1920s by an enterprising boat captain, Dells attractions
were expanded by the even more enterprising Crandall
sisters, Phyllis and Lois, into a terrific Indian entertainment show. These fabulous ladies also purchased the
seven-mile stretch of riverfront and willed its ancient
beauty to the University of Wisconsin.

Downtown Wisconsin Dells and U.S. 12 through the
town of Lake Delton contain most of the hotel rooms,
shops, tourist attractions (like Wax World, Ripley's,
Noah's Ark water park, Biblical Gardens, fun parks,
museums), restaurants, souvenir shops, greyhound rac-
ing, and entertainments for kids of all ages. Pick up a
*Wisconsin Dells: The Fun Comes Naturally* catalog of
things to see and do at the Visitor and Convention
Bureau, 701 Superior Street, in Wisconsin Dells, or any-

where in town. You'll have a choice of thousands of guest rooms, seven bed and breakfasts, more than 20 campgrounds with almost 3,000 campsites, and a few hundred restaurants.

▲▲▲ **The Upper Dells Tour**—With landings at three scenic places (Stand Rock, Witches Gulch, and Cold Water Canyon), the Upper Dells tour takes 2½ hours and costs $10.50. The Stand Rock Indian Ceremonial can be reached by a boat that leaves at 7:45 p.m. and costs $12.45 for adults and children. The Lower Dells boat trip is a one-hour, nonstop tour featuring the Rocky Islands and costs $6.85. The combined Upper and Lower Dells boat trip costs $13.65. From mid-May to mid-October, boats leave Upper and Lower Falls docks every 20 minutes from 8:00 a.m. to 7:00 p.m. The Olson Boat Co., (608) 254-8500, in downtown Wisconsin Dells, The Dells Boat Co., (608) 253-1561, at the Railroad Bridge, and the Riverview Boat Line, (608) 254-8336, at the junction of Highways 12 and 16, offer all of the Dells' boat tours. Dells Boat Tours, which represents all of these companies, has produced a useful price list for all attractions in the Dells.

▲ **The Ducks**—These World War II amphibious landing crafts maneuver through scenic forests, hills, and valleys and then into the Wisconsin River for a glimpse of the Lower Dells. Try the Ducks for a waker-upper before leaving Wisconsin Dells. The fare is $9.75 for adults, $3 for children under 12. The Wisconsin Ducks berth one mile south of Wisconsin Dells on Highway 12.

## Lodging
**The Historic Bennett House**, 825 Oak Street, Wisconsin Dells, (608) 254-2500, was built in 1863 and purchased by famous nature photographer H. H. Bennett in 1891. Gail and Rich Obermeyer bought the house in 1988 and beautifully redecorated it. Available for guests are a downstairs suite with a sitting room and private shower ($85) and two lovely upstairs rooms with a shared bath (each $60). Delicious full breakfasts are served in the dining room.

**The Sherman House B&B**, 930 River Road, Wisconsin Dells, (608) 253-2721, is two blocks from downtown on a hill overlooking the Wisconsin River. This estate house with eight bedrooms was designed with the picturesque view of the river in mind. Overlooking the river is the large veranda where Norma Marz serves a full breakfast. A double room with shared bath costs only $45. Turn right on Wisconsin from River Road and left on the first alley, drive to the park at the end, and the house is on your left.

For a very decent standard room, suite, or family unit, the **Indian Trail Motel**, 1013 East Broadway, Wisconsin Dells, (608) 253-2641, is an excellent choice at $55 for one bed, one or two persons, and $70 for up to four persons and two double beds. There is a large pool on the grounds.

## Camping

Three miles from Wisconsin Dells, **Mirror Lake State Park**, E10320 Ferndell Road, Baraboo, WI 53913, (608) 254-2333, has 144 wooded campsites, 27 with electricity. Among the three campgrounds within the park, Cliffwood and Blue Water Bay have showers. Reservations are essential between Memorial Day and Labor Day, especially over weekends and for campsites with electrical hookups. Half of Mirror Lake, which has excellent fishing and swimming, is surrounded by scenic sandstone bluffs, resembling Devil's Lake. Drive ½ mile south of I-90/94 on U.S. 22, then west on Ferndell Road for 1½ miles to **Rocky Arbor State Park**, c/o Mirror Lake State Park, E10320 Ferndell Rd., Baraboo, WI 53913. This park is eight miles from Mirror Lake, 1½ miles north of the Dells on Highway 12. Tucked away in beautiful white and Norway pines, this 225-acre park has soaring rock formations around its 89 wooded campsites. Only 18 have electrical hookups.

Both suggested campgrounds on Highway 12 are on your right as you drive north. **KOA Wisconsin**, is ½ mile north of the Dells at S235P Standrock Road, (608)

254-4177. There are 98 campsites and the nightly fee is
$17 plus $2.50 for electricity. Showers are available.
**Stand Rock Campground**, with 140 spacious campsites
spread over 100 acres, charges $16 plus $2.50 for electricity. Showers are available, and there is a camp store
and a coin-operated laundry. The campground is
2 ½ miles north of Highway 12 on Stand Rock Road
(Highway N), halfway between the Dells and the Stand
Rock Ceremonial. The address is N570 Highway N,
Wisconsin Dells, 53965, (608) 253-2169.

## Food

**Suzie's Restaurant**, 146 4th Avenue, corner of 4th and
Broadway, Baraboo, (608) 356-9911, has delicious pasta
specials daily. Everything on the lunch and brunch menu,
such as stir-fry vegetables, omelets with sauteed mushrooms and white wine sauce, croissant French toast with
orange and triple sec, and fresh muffins, is gourmet
standard, to my knowledge unsurpassed by any small restaurant in the Great Lakes. The very pleasing decor, wonderful atmosphere, and inexpensive dishes are the work
of Sue Quiriconi, one of the most delightful persons I've
ever encountered in the restaurant business.

The Dells has more than 40 decent restaurants and
other eateries, so you won't go hungry. Most of them are
on Highway 12 from I-94/I-90 to Broadway (Highway
23). Since 1925, good, inexpensive home-cooked food
has been served at the unpretentious **Patio Restaurant**,
208 Broadway, Wisconsin Dells, (608) 254-7178. Another
family-operated restaurant (since 1950), **Fisher's Restaurant**, U.S. 12 in Lake Delton, (608) 253-7531, is a basic
family-style steak, prime rib, and seafood place with its
own down-home baking.

# WISCONSIN DELLS TO STURGEON BAY

Drive from the Wisconsin Dells to Sturgeon Bay at the base of Door Peninsula by way of Oshkosh, Appleton, and Green Bay. Bypass Green Bay today and visit it on the way north on Day 9. In Oshkosh on Lake Winnebago, visit the Experimental Aircraft Association (EAA) Museum or take a riverboat cruise on the Fox River. Anglers may not be able to resist the temptation to fish for perch, walleye, sturgeon, and other lake fish. If you have time, see Oshkosh's Grand Opera House and the Paine Art Center and Arboretum. Arrive in Sturgeon Bay for dinner and check in at one of the city's exceptional historic B&Bs.

## Suggested Schedule

| | |
|---|---|
| 8:30 a.m. | Leisurely breakfast and check-out. |
| 10:00 a.m. | Drive to Oshkosh. |
| 12:00 noon | Arrive at Oshkosh's EAA Museum. |
| 12:30 p.m. | Lunch at the EAA Museum and tour the museum. |
| 4:00 p.m. | Leave for Sturgeon Bay. |
| 6:00 p.m. | Arrive in Sturgeon Bay and check in. |
| 7:00 p.m. | Stroll and dinner. |

### Travel Route: Wisconsin Dells to Sturgeon Bay (174 miles)

From the Wisconsin Dells to Oshkosh and Appleton is 101 miles, and from Appleton to Green Bay and then to Sturgeon Bay is 73 miles. Take I-51 to WI 23 East to Ripon and then WI 44 to Oshkosh. Just as you cross Highway 41, Highway 44 becomes Knapps Street. On your right is Poberezny Road, which leads to the entrance to the EAA Aviation Center on your left. When you return to Highway 41, you're 60 minutes from Green Bay and 43 miles on Highway 57 to Sturgeon Bay (allow one hour). Plan to see Green Bay on Day 9.

## Sightseeing Highlights

▲ **Oshkosh**—The city might be best known for its Oshkosh B'Gosh overalls and other clothing, but the EAA museum is the area's leading tourist attraction. A live performance at the beautiful **Grand Opera House**, (414) 236-5290, and the 14-acre botanical gardens and elegant museum of the **Paine Art Center and Arboretum**, (414) 235-4530, are well worth seeing if you have the time.

▲▲ **Experimental Aircraft Association (EAA) Air Adventure Museum**—Located at the EAA Aviation Center, 3000 Poberezny Drive, (414) 426-4818, the museum has more than 80 aircraft on display. The largest private collection in the world, it includes antiques, ultralights, military planes from World War II, barnstorming planes, racers, and a fascinating assortment of other planes that have been flown for every imaginable purpose. Hours are Monday through Saturday from 8:30 a.m. to 5:00 p.m., Sunday 11:00 a.m. to 5:00 p.m. Adult admission is $5, children $4. The EAA Air Adventure Theater shows *On the Wing,* an excellent film about every aspect of flight. The EAA Fly-In Convention in late July and early August is the world's largest aviation event, attracting more than 15,000 planes and 20 or 30 times as many people. Hundreds of lectures, workshops, and informal events are offered. If you plan to attend this event, book lodgings well ahead in Oshkosh or the surrounding area.

## Lodging

As you'll find throughout northern Wisconsin and Michigan's Upper Peninsula in summer or "high" season, many of the innkeepers require a minimum two-day or longer stay and many cottage owners require a one-week minimum stay in July and August. Some inns, restaurants, and shops are closed during the winter. There are no large chain hotels in Door County. Most places are family owned and operated. Many B&Bs accept only adult guests or children over a minimum age. Smoking is not permitted or is restricted to certain locations at most small inns.

Bill and Fran Cecil's **The Scofield House**, 908 Michigan Street, Sturgeon Bay, WI 54235, (414) 743-7727, is "precious Queen Anne-style Victorian" with tasteful concessions to twentieth-century comfort such as central air-conditioning, stereo systems, and videos. The owners, a former hospital administrator and a nurse, share the same vision of luxurious comfort for this B&B, elegantly furnished with 1800s antiques, and with all private baths. The Rose Room features a double whirlpool bath, and the Turret Suite has a double shower. Guests enjoy a full gourmet breakfast served in the gazebo and can relax on a front porch swing. The four guest rooms cost $60 to $110 per night.

Dennis and Bonnie Statz's **The White Lace Inn**, 16 N. Fifth Avenue, Sturgeon Bay, WI 54235, (414) 743-1105, comprises three restored historic homes connected by beautiful gardens. When you enter the front door of the main house, you'll likely be greeted by the fragrance of fresh lilacs and the sweet aroma of breakfast treats baking and Scandinavian fruit soup simmering. The inn has fourteen guest rooms, all with private baths and beautifully appointed with fireplaces, fine period antiques, four-poster canopy or Victorian beds, the best linens, good lighting, and, of course, delicate touches of white lace. Many rooms have queen-size beds and double whirlpool baths; one room has a two-sided fireplace and a raised double-whirlpool bath for the ultimate in romantic indulgence. Rates are $78 to $135 double.

## Camping
Campers have the option of staying overnight in one of **Potawatomi State Park**'s 125 wooded campsites (23 with electrical hookups). Half the campsites can be reserved. Reservations are essential in July and August and on autumn weekends. You'll find more than six miles of hiking trails. The park operates year-round and has the only downhill ski slope in Door County. It is four miles southwest of Sturgeon Bay. Take Highway 42/57 and fol-

low the signs to Park Drive. For reservations, write the park at 3740 Park Drive, Sturgeon Bay, WI 54235, (414) 743-8869 or -8860. (See Sightseeing Highlights, Day 7.)

In a lovely wooded area, **Quietwoods North**, 3668 Grondin Road, Sturgeon Bay, WI 54235, (414) 743-7115, toll-free out-of-state, (800) 472-3677, toll-free in Wisconsin, (800) 742-9305, is a campers' resort. It offers 200 campsites with electricity, two large heated pools, showers, water and sewer sites, recreation building, store, and more for $18 per night, plus $2.50 for electricity. Drive north on Duluth Avenue, turn left on County Highway C, then right on Grondin Road. If you continue driving on Grondin Road, you will see signs directing you to Potawatomi State Park.

**Food**

The **Inn at Cedar Crossing**, 336 Louisiana Street, Sturgeon Bay, (414) 743-4200, has a menu full of exceptionally delicious fare, including rich, unforgettable soups that are a meal in a bowl, and breads and pastries baked daily. Hours are Monday through Saturday 7:00 a.m. to 9:00 p.m., Sunday 7:30 a.m. to 1:30 p.m. The **White Birch Inn**, 1009 S. Oxford, (414) 743-3295, across from the Quarterdeck Marina in Sturgeon Bay, serves daily specials featuring steaks, perch, whitefish, and chicken. The Old Southwest decor and fireplace make it a pleasant place for lunch, served 11:30 a.m. to 2:00 p.m., or dinner, served 5:30 to 9:30 p.m. daily.

# DOOR PENINSULA

Door County's peninsula is famous for its beautiful shorelines on Lake Michigan and especially on the Green Bay
coast, which are dotted with quaint historic towns—Egg
Harbor, Fish Creek, Ephraim, Sister Bay, and others.
Nearby Washington Island and Rock Island are reached
by ferries from the peninsula's tip. State parks—Potawatomi, Peninsula, Newport, and Whitefish Dunes—
compare with any in the Great Lakes for beautiful forests,
wilderness trails, and lakefront beaches. The scenic
beauty of the peninsula's interior is equally a focus of the
next two days. You'll enjoy cherry and apple orchards
along delightful country roads and several unforgettable
nature preserves on the Lake Michigan coast.

## Suggested Schedule

| | |
|---|---|
| 7:30 a.m. | Breakfast in Sturgeon Bay and check out. |
| 8:30 a.m. | Visit Potawatomi State Park. |
| 9:00 a.m. | Tour Peninsula State Park. |
| 12:00 noon | Lunch, sightseeing, and shopping in Fish Creek. |
| 2:30 p.m. | Drive through Ephraim to Sister Bay and Ellison Bay to Gill's Rock. |
| 4:00 p.m. | Refreshment break in Rowley's Harbor. |
| 4:30 p.m. | Drive through Bailey's Harbor and Jacksonport. |
| 6:30 p.m. | Return to Fish Creek, where you'll spend two nights. |
| 8:30 p.m. | Fish boil dinner in Fish Creek. |

**Travel Route: Sturgeon Bay to Fish Creek (23 miles)**
Drive southwest of Sturgeon Bay on Highway 42/57 to
Park Drive and Potawatomi State Park, then retrace your
route back to Highway 42 north. Drive up the peninsula
along the Green Bay coast from Sturgeon Bay to Egg
Harbor, Fish Creek, through Peninsula State Park, to

## Door Peninsula/Washington and Rock Islands

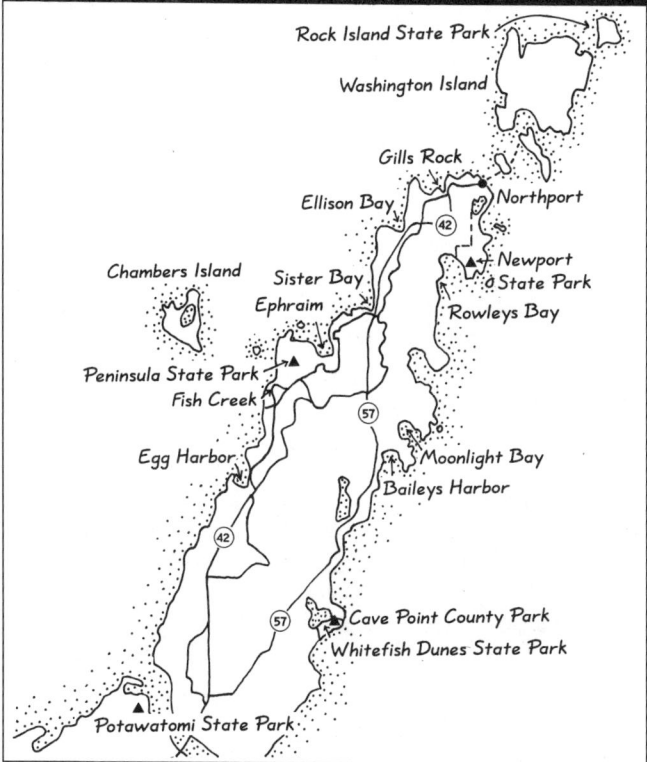

Rock Island State Park

Washington Island

Gills Rock

Ellison Bay

Northport

(42)

Newport
State Park

Chambers Island

Sister Bay

Ephraim

Rowleys Bay

Peninsula State Park
Fish Creek

(57)

Egg Harbor

Moonlight Bay
Baileys Harbor

(42)

(57)

Cave Point County Park
Whitefish Dunes State Park

Potawatomi State Park

historic Ephraim, following Shore Road to Sister Bay,
Beach Road and Porcupine Bay Road to Garrett Bay Road,
and Cottage Road to Gill's Rock and Northpoint, where
tomorrow you'll take the car ferry to Washington Island.
From Northpoint, make a right turn on Timberline Road
to Newport Beach State Park. Return to Ellison Bay on
Newport Road to pick up Mink River Road to Rowley's
Bay on Lake Michigan.

Grandma's Bakery at the Wagon Trail Resort in Rowley's
Bay is reached on County Highway ZZ. After your break,
continue on County Highway ZZ toward Sister Bay to get
on Woodcrest Road to County Highway Q, which goes to

Cana Island, across Moonlight Bay to Bailey's Harbor. The Bailey's Harbor area offers wonderful natural protected areas around Moonlight Bay, the Mud Lake Wildlife Area, and the Ridges Sanctuary. From Bailey's Harbor, take County Highway F back to Fish Creek.

## Door Peninsula

The 42-mile-long, 13-mile-wide Door Peninsula has two distinct coasts, though they are only a few miles apart: the **Green Bay coast**, warmer and more protected from Lake Michigan's water and weather, and the **Lake Michigan coast**, where it is not unusual to find the weather 5 to 10 degrees cooler and foggy when the Green Bay side is sunny and clear. By far the best sand beaches are on the Lake Michigan coast at Newport and Whitefish Bay state parks.

Few of the county trunk roads on the narrow peninsula carry heavy traffic, even on holiday weekends. Everywhere there are cherry and apple orchards and rolling meadows bounded by stone fences. Door County is the land of milk and fruit, with small farms on stony soil growing crops to feed milk cows. Coastal side roads lead to marshy lowlands and lakes filled with waterfowl. Many original mid-nineteenth-century buildings still stand in coastal villages. Much hard work and loving care have converted some of these charming Victorian structures into B&Bs.

## Sightseeing Highlights

▲▲▲ **Potawatomi State Park**—Located at the entrance to Sturgeon Bay, the park's rugged limestone cliffs provide wonderful seascapes as an introduction to Door Peninsula, Green Bay, and northern Lake Michigan. A 75-foot observation tower stands 225 feet over the bay. On a clear day you can see Chambers Island, 20 miles to the northeast, and across the bay to some of your next

destinations—Marinette, Wisconsin, and Menominee,
Michigan, 16 miles across Green Bay.

▲▲▲ **Peninsula State Park**—Adjoining the north side
of Fish Creek, Peninsula State Park, P.O. Box 218, Fish
Creek, WI 54212, (414) 868-3258, also can be reached
from the Ephraim side. Thousands of acres of native
hardwood forests give you a glimpse of how Door
County and the north woods looked before the era of settlement and logging. From 75 feet up **Eagle Tower**, view
Ephraim's two white steeples echoing each other on a
hillside across the sparkling harbor, far from the usual din
surrounding Wilson's Ice Cream parlor on Ephraim's
shorefront.

You can drive for 20 miles through the woods, hike for
19 miles, or ski on groomed and marked cross-country
ski trails, or bicycle on 9 miles of designated bike routes.
Be sure to bike the 5.5-mile **Sunset Trail**. At the Fish
Creek entrance you can rent bicycles. **Nicolet Bay**'s sand
beach is excellent for swimming. Come in May for brown
trout, perch, walleye, or smallmouth bass fishing or to see
spring warbler migrations. (See Camping, below.)

## Lodging

Ozzie and Violet Senzel have run **Tip Top Cottages**,
9709 Highway 42, Fish Creek, WI 54212, (414) 854-2228,
for more than 40 years. Ozzie is a master craftsman. His
carpentry work includes handmade furniture and cabine-
try in all the cottages. The decor is charming—goldfish
wall decorations in the bath and a collection of knick-
knacks that covers the spectrum. Each of the half-dozen
cottages is equipped with everything—from cooking
utensils to bathroom supplies—and they're super-clean.
Ozzie and Violet are wonderful, hospitable, caring people. The property adjoins the golf course and couldn't be
better for biking or hiking in Peninsula State Park. This is
a great place for families. Rates are $65 to $85 per cottage,
double occupancy in season.

**The Whistling Swan**, P.O. Box 193, Fish Creek, WI
54212, (414) 868-3442, is at the heart of Fish Creek's

historic section. Looking at this large inn, you'll be as astonished as I was to learn that it was built in Marinette, Wisconsin, in 1887, and shortly after the turn of the century, Dr. Herman Welcker had it set on logs and drawn by horses across frozen Green Bay and erected on its present site. It became Dr. Welcker's Casino and part of Welcker's resort properties that included the White Gull Inn a few blocks away. In 1986, Jan and Andy Coulson completely renovated the inn's four bedrooms and three suites with sitting rooms, all on the second floor and with private baths. The Whistling Swan shop is on the first floor. Across the street is Founders Square with a variety of shops and restaurants. The neighborhood is ideal for strolling to Sunset Park, which overlooks Green Bay. The inn is open from May through October and Christmas week, weekends throughout the rest of the year. Rates range from $80 to $124.

Since 1972, the Coulsons have owned the **White Gull Inn**, P.O. Box 159, Fish Creek, WI 54212, (414) 868-3517, Door County's oldest country inn. The White Gull is open year-round. Ten rooms vary from those with shared baths to elegant, spacious rooms with private bathrooms and fireplaces. Rates are double bed/private bath, $64 to $78; double or twin bed with shared bath, $40 to $52.

**Camping**
Besides Peninsula State Park, there are several excellent private campgrounds in the Egg Harbor area for RVers and other campers. **Frontier Wilderness Campground**, 4375 Hillside Road, Egg Harbor, WI 54209, (414) 868-3349, offers a heated indoor pool, first-rate sauna, private shower stalls and washrooms, and 127 drive-up and walk-in RV, camper, and tent sites. Two miles before Egg Harbor on Highway 42, turn right for 1½ miles on Hillside Road. The nightly rate is $12 per couple with electricity and water, $2 per child, and $2 less with no hookups. **Camp-tel Family Campground**, 8164 Highway 42, Egg Harbor, WI 54209, (414) 868-3278,

has about the same rates and 93 attractive wooded sites
1½ miles north of Egg Harbor on Highway 42.

**Peninsula State Park**, P.O. Box 218, Fish Creek, WI
54212, (414) 868-3258, off Highway 42 at the north end
of Fish Creek, has 472 campsites in four campgrounds.
All have showers, but only 100 have electricity. Reservations are essential in July and August and on autumn
weekends. For every type of outdoor recreation, this is
one of the best parks in the Great Lakes.

**Food**

**The Cookery Restaurant**, Main Street, Fish Creek, (414)
868-3634, serves breakfast, lunch, and dinner. Specialties
include omelets, whitefish chowder, unique sandwiches,
nightly specials, and desserts made on the premises.
Open daily from April through October; in winter, on
weekends only.

**The Wagon Trail Resort** on the west coast, 1041 CH
ZZ, (414) 854-2385, nestled on the shore of Rowley's Bay,
is a family recreational resort with an indoor pool, game
room, boats, canoes, bicycles, tennis, hiking and jogging,
cross-country skiing, exercise equipment, whirlpool,
sauna, and so on. Its restaurant, **Grandma's Bakery**,
serves great burlap bread, cherry muffins, and a big buffet lunch with very good soups.

**The Cottage Restaurant** on Highway 42 in the center
of Sister Bay, (414) 854-2429, serves good breakfasts if
you're not in a hurry and desserts worth waiting for even
if you are, such as pioneer bread pudding, rhubarb torte,
and Myrtle's cream cheese pie.

**The White Gull Inn**, 4225 Main Street, Fish Creek,
(414) 868-3517, serves breakfast, lunch, and dinner daily
year-round. The fish boil is reputedly the best in Door
County, even though, in violation of tradition, the unique
White Gull recipe does not include onions. A fish boil is
Door County's most famous tradition, and every restaurant and inn promotes its own. This outdoor event
features a local fish boil expert building a fire under a
huge caldron of water and tossing in large hunks of Lake

Michigan whitefish. The brew simmers for hours with seasoning, onions, and potatoes. At some point, it boils over, and the fish fat is skimmed off in the boiling foam. The White Gull's garden is a great spot to see the sunset and watch the caldron as the master boiler prepares the whitefish just as it was done 100 years ago by Scandinavian settlers of the peninsula. The meal includes delicious cole slaw, homemade bread, and Door County cherry pie.

RVers and other travelers will want to stock up at **Bea's Ho-made Products**, 42 Gills Rock, Ellison Bay, (414) 854-2268, a half mile east of Gills Rock on a farm that has been owned by the Landin family since 1884. Their canning business started by chance in 1962, when daughter Linda started selling cherries on a picnic table by the roadside. Inspired by her success with cherry sales, she expanded to selling cherry jam made by her grandmother, then pickles, relish, and other treats from the farm kitchen. Bea's is open seven days a week May 15 through November 1, 8:00 a.m. to 5:00 p.m. Monday through Saturday, and 10:00 a.m. to 4:30 p.m. on Sunday.

# DOOR PENINSULA AND
# WASHINGTON ISLAND

Spend more time touring the roads and trails of Peninsula State Park, the shoreside, and the beach. Drive through Ephraim, Sister Bay, Ellison Bay, and Gills Rock to Northport Pier Ferry Dock for the ferry to Washington Island. Leave your car in Northpoint, or take it with you if you plan to drive on Washington Island rather than rent a bicycle. On Washington Island, rent bicycles near Detroit Harbor's dock for an afternoon of touring Washington Island and Rock Island State Park. Return to the peninsula on one of the last ferries and have dinner in Bailey's Harbor before heading back to Fish Creek.

## Suggested Schedule

| | |
|---|---|
| 8:00 a.m. | Breakfast in Fish Creek. |
| 9:00 a.m. | Tour Peninsula State Park. |
| 10:30 a.m. | Drive to Northport for ferry to Washington Island and Rock Island. |
| 12:30 p.m. | Picnic lunch on Washington Island or ferry from Jackson Harbor to Rock Island. |
| 2:00 p.m. | Recreation on Washington Island or Rock Island. |
| 5:00 p.m. | Return to Door Peninsula. |
| 7:00 p.m. | Drive to Bailey's Harbor for dinner and sunset. |

## Sightseeing Highlights
▲ **Washington Island Excursion**—At the top of Door's thumb thrash the turbulent straits between Door Peninsula and Washington Island. The waters have gobbled up the likes of Ottawa Indian war parties, Robert La Salle Griffin's schooner, which was the first to sail the Great Lakes, and hundreds of other vessels and their crews. From the point aptly named "Death Door," Door Bluff Headlands County Park at the end of a logging trail

overlooks ferries that connect Washington Island and the
mainland at Gills Rock ($6.50 round-trip for your auto,
$2.50 for adult passengers, $1.50 for children 6 to 11,
50 cents for bicycles, and $3 for motorcycles). Between
July 1 and August 31, the ferry leaves for Washington
Island every 30 minutes starting at 7:15 a.m., and the last
ferry returns at 6:00 p.m. For more information, call (414)
847-2546.

   A bracing 7-mile, 40-minute ferry trip past Plum Island
and Pilot Island ends at the dock at Lobdells Point in
Detroit Harbor. Gift shops cluster around the harbor.
Don't worry, the rest of the island has little commercial
development. Bicycles are for rent in the harbor. Cyclers
on all-terrain bikes or undaunted thin-wheelers can
enjoy undeveloped forestland from unpaved, rough
roads on the eastern side of the island. Follow Main Road
and then take a right turn on Jackson Harbor Road and
proceed through farmland and forest to Jackson Harbor
and the Rock Island ferry.

**▲▲▲ Rock Island Excursion**—With no motorized
vehicles of any sort allowed, Rock Island State Park is a
very special place where you can hike around the island
in about three hours or take shorter trails to the cliffs at
Potowatomi Lighthouse, the first lighthouse on the Great
Lakes, or to the half mile of beach on the south shore.
You can mountain bike on 11 miles of trails, with some
rough spots. Once the private estate of Chester Thordar-
son, an inventor born in Iceland, the impressive stone
boathouse and Viking hall with its historic artifacts are
open to the public. The park has 40 primitive campsites,
some a few steps from Lake Michigan. Bring your own
supplies if you intend to camp since there are no stores
on the island. Reservations for campsites can be made
from May 1 to September 1 through Rock Island State
Park Headquarters, Washington Island, WI 54246, (414)
847-2235.

   The **KARFI** ferry, (414) 847-2425, leaves Jackson
Harbor for the fifteen-minute trip to Rock Island. Fares
are: $4 adults, $3 children, $5 campers with gear, and $2

bicycles. June 30 through September 4, the ferry departs every hour on the hour, 10:00 a.m. to 4:00 p.m. daily. From May 26 through June 29 and September 5 through the end of October, it runs 9:00 a.m., 10:00 a.m., 1:00 p.m., and 3:30 p.m. daily, with extra trips on weekends and Memorial Day.

## Itinerary Options

**Bailey's Harbor–Fish Creek**—In **Lighthouse Point Nature Preserve**, just north of Bailey's Harbor and off County Trunk Q, wildflowers and birds inhabit a series of sixteen ancient shorelines formed by Ice Age glaciers. This area is preserved as **The Ridges Sanctuary**, (414) 839-2802, a 910-acre area of wooded bogs, sandy ridges, swales, and Lake Michigan beach. It is a wonderful complex of rare wildflowers, wildlife, and unusual ecological communities and extensive trail and boardwalk systems. Moonlight Bay's Cana Island Road leads to Cana Island Lighthouse, one of sixteen lighthouses overlooking the treacherous reefs and shoals of Lake Michigan's Door County shoreline.

**Bailey's Harbor to Egg Harbor to Fish Creek**—From Bailey's Harbor, cyclers or vehicles can return to Ephraim on East Point Road or Sunset Road to County Trunk Q, then down the very steep hill into Ephraim. Take County E past Kangaroo Lake to any one of several small roads passing acres of sour Montmorency cherry orchards that thrive on the peninsula's milder winters and slower springs. Make your way over to coastal County Trunks B and G leading north to Egg Harbor and Fish Creek.

## Food

**Bailey's Harbor Yacht Club and Resort**, (414-839-2336), located off Highway 57 at Bailey's Harbor, has beautiful views of the sunset from its dining room and Bayview Lounge. While you soak up the view, chef Willy will look after your dining requirements. Monday through Saturday year-round, breakfast starts at 7:00 a.m. and dinner service stops at 10:00 p.m. Boiled, broiled, and fried fish are the restaurant's specialties.

## DAY 9
# GREEN BAY TO MARINETTE AND MENOMINEE

Wisconsin's oldest city, founded in 1669, is most famous for its football team. At the Packer Hall of Fame, you can share the emotion that made the Green Bay Packers a perennial powerhouse in the Vince Lombardi days. At Heritage Hill State Park, see the reality of eighteenth- and nineteenth-century Wisconsin life. Drive along the coast of Green Bay to the border cities of Marinette, Wisconsin, and Menominee, Michigan.

### Suggested Schedule

| | |
|---|---|
| 7:30 a.m. | Breakfast. |
| 8:30 a.m. | Leave Fish Creek for Green Bay. |
| 10:30 a.m. | Arrive in Green Bay. |
| 11:00 a.m. | See Heritage Hill State Park. |
| 1:00 p.m. | Lunch. |
| 3:00 p.m. | See Packer Hall of Fame. |
| 4:30 p.m. | Leave for Marinette and Menominee. |
| 6:00 p.m. | Arrive in Marinette/Menominee area and check into lodgings. |
| 6:30 p.m. | If camping, continue to J. W. Wells State Park. |

**Travel Route: Fish Creek to Marinette and Menominee (115 miles)**

From Fish Creek take Highway 42 south to Sturgeon Bay and then Highway 57 along the Green Bay coast to Green Bay, a total of 75 miles. In Green Bay, from Highway 57 take Highway 43 south to Highway 172 west to Webster Avenue. Exit on the north (right) side of Highway 172. Heritage Hill State Park is right there. After visiting the park, get back on Highway 172 west to Highway 41 north, exit at Lombardi east (right), and you're at Lambeau Field. Return to Highway 41 north to Marinette and Menominee, a distance of 55 miles and slightly over an hour's drive.

## Door Peninsula and Green Bay Region

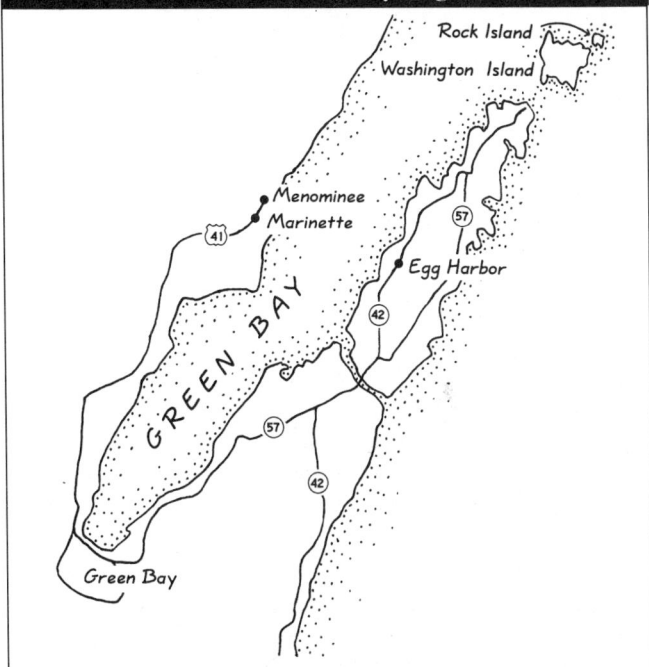

Private camping is very sparse in the Marinette/Menominee area, so I suggest that RVers and campers continue another 23 miles to J. W. Wells State Park on M-35, a beautiful route along the Lake Michigan shore to Escanaba. Others can stay in Menominee on the Michigan side of the Menominee River.

### Sightseeing Highlights

▲▲ **Heritage Hill State Park**—A 40-acre site sloping to the Fox River is the setting for 22 buildings dating to the 1770s which have been restored and grouped in four theme areas. The Pioneer Heritage Area covers three eras, with exhibits like a seventeenth-century Jesuit bark chapel, an eighteenth-century fur trader's cabin, and an early nineteenth- century sugar mapling house and a courthouse. The Military Heritage Area depicts frontier military life at Fort Howard circa 1836. The Small Town Heritage Area shows eighteenth- and nineteenth-century small town homes and other buildings. The Agricultural/ Ethnic Heritage Area includes a turn-of-the-century Belgian immigrant farming community. Interpreters in costume create the characters of blacksmiths, school teachers, fur traders, farmers, soldiers, voyageurs reenact- ing a fur trade rendezvous, and other figures of these periods. Open 10 a.m. to 5:00 p.m. on weekends in May and September and Tuesday through Sunday from Memorial Day to Labor Day. Admission is $4 for adults, $2 for children under 19, and $10 per family. The address is 2640 S. Webster, telephone (414) 497-4268.

▲▲ **The Packer Hall of Fame**—Two floors and a gift shop are filled with every imaginable bit of Packer and NFL memorabilia, making the legends of Lombardi, Lambeau, Hornung, Hutson, and others come alive. Even fans of other pro football teams will be moved by films of Packer moments of triumph and coach Vince Lom- bardi's great gap-toothed smile. For fun, anyone can try his hand at throwing a pass or kicking a field goal in a padded area of the museum set aside for such antics. Admission is $4 for adults, $2.50 for children under 13, and $14 per family. Open daily 10:00 a.m. to 5:00 p.m., 1901 S. Oneida Street, across from Lambeau Field and Lombardi Avenue, (414) 499-4281.

▲ **Peshtigo Fire Museum**—Six miles southwest of Marinette, you'll drive through Peshtigo. If there's time, see the Peshtigo Fire Museum housed in the first church constructed after the disastrous Peshtigo fire of 1871. This spectacular fire destroyed the entire city and killed more than 800 people on the same day that Chicago's much more famous fire killed 20 people. Burning a million acres of land as far south as Green Bay, across to Door County and north to Menominee, this was the worst for- est fire in American history. A large portion of the museum is devoted to the fire, but there are other histori-

cal displays. Open June through October, 9:00 a.m. to
5:00 p.m.; admission is free, but donations are accepted.
The museum is on Oconto Avenue. One block north of
U.S. 41, turn at Ellis Street, then Oconto (715) 582-9995.

## Lodging

In Menominee is Sherry and Steve Homa's **Lauerman
Guest House Inn**, 1975 Riverside Avenue, (715)
732-7800, a Victorian-style B&B. All seven guest rooms
have private baths and share the mansion's beautiful
rooms with mahogany, black walnut, oak, and bird's-eye
maple paneling. Two rooms in this three-story house
have whirlpools. Rates start at $68 double. Downtown
Marinette, across the river, is only three blocks away. The
Homas serve excellent lunches and dinners to nonguests
as well as guests. Reservations are requested. Just a block
away, the **Best Western Riverside Inn**, 1821 Riverside
Avenue, Menominee, (715) 732-0111, is the big new hotel
in town. Rates for a double room start at $65.

## Camping

Located on Green Bay, 23 miles north of Menominee and
one mile south of Cedar River, 975-acre **J. W. Wells State
Park** has 166 large, modern, grassy campsites, with 32
sites (even-numbered 6-64) right on the three-mile shoreline. Every site has some shade trees. Six rustic frontier
cabins can be rented year-round. Seven miles of trails are
lined with virgin pine, maple, beech, hemlock, and bass-
wood and surrounded by cedar, birch, spruce, and elm.
J. W. Wells State Park, M-35, Cedar River, MI 49813, (906)
863-9747.

## Food

**Shloegel's Restaurant**, 1828 Hall Avenue on U.S. 41 in
Marinette, and also in Menominee, (715) 863-7888, open
Monday through Saturday, 6:00 a.m. to 10:00 p.m., is
unsurpassed in either city for tasty, moderately priced
meals. The **Brothers Three Pizza**, 1302 Marinette Avenue, Marinette, (715) 735-9054, specializes in delicious

pizzas (try the veggie supreme) but also offers an amazing
assortment of inexpensive lunches and dinners including
Italian, Mexican, sandwiches, fish, beef, chicken, and
salads. Hours are 11:00 a.m. to 11:00 p.m., Monday
through Saturday. In Menominee's historic downtown is
the **Waterfront Restaurant**, operated by the owners of
the Best Western Riverside Inn. The Waterfront, at 450
First Street, (906) 863-1218, serves expensive but very
good meals.

## MENOMINEE TO ESCANABA AND FAYETTE STATE PARK

History buffs can see an important chapter in the story of the Upper Peninsula's logging era of the 1800s and early 1900s on Stephenson Island on the Wisconsin-Michigan border, as they cross into Michigan for the short drive to Menominee's waterfront historic district. Drive on M-35 along the beautiful Green Bay coast—to an outdoor recreation wonderland. Continue to the beautiful Garden Peninsula to see the totally intact, picturesque ghost town of Fayette.

### Suggested Schedule

| | |
|---|---|
| 8:00 a.m. | Breakfast and check-out. |
| 9:00 a.m. | Stop at the Michigan Tourist Information Center in Menominee. |
| 9:30 a.m. | Stroll in Menominee's waterfront historic district. |
| 10:00 a.m. | See the Marinette County Logging Museum. |
| 10:30 a.m. | Drive along M-35 to Escanaba. |
| 12:00 noon | Lunch in Escanaba. |
| 1:00 p.m. | Visit Delta County Historical Museum and Lighthouse. |
| 2:00 p.m. | Drive to Fayette State Park. |
| 3:00 p.m. | Arrive in Fayette and tour the town. |
| 5:00 p.m. | Check into campsite or drive to other accommodations. |
| 6:00 p.m. | Dinner. |

### Travel Route: Menominee to Escanaba to Fayette (107 miles)

Welcome to Michigan. Continue a few blocks on Highway 41 to the Michigan Tourist Information Center at the corner of Highway 41 and 10th Avenue for maps and a wealth of information on Michigan for the next part of your trip. Follow 1st Street to the Menominee historic

waterfront district, then return to the bridge to Marinette
to visit the Logging Museum when it opens at 10:00 a.m.
Afterward, drive on U.S. 41 again to M-35 to Escanaba,
return to U.S. 41 to Rapid River where you'll pick up U.S.
2 and drive to the turnoff for the Garden Peninsula at
C-183. Drive 17 miles down the Garden Peninsula to
Fayette State Park. Stay overnight, and the next day head
to Munising via Palms Book State Park and its unique
spring, Kitch-iti-ki-pi, and Manistique.

**Sightseeing Highlights**
▲ **First Street Historic District**—Menominee, the
lumbering center of the Upper Peninsula, contains a
historic district between 10th and 4th avenues that is the
setting for a waterfront festival each July. A variety of
shops occupy restored nineteenth-century waterfront
buildings. Continue on 10th Avenue to the Menominee
County Historical Museum on Second Street.
▲ **Marinette County Logging Museum**—On Stephenson Island between Marinette and Menominee, the Logging
Museum, (715) 732-0831, commemorates the people
who worked in the woods from 1856 to 1917, cutting and
processing more than 10 billion feet of timber. A carefully
crafted miniature replica of an old logging camp is
equipped with tools of the era. Open late May through
September, Monday through Saturday 10:00 a.m. to
4:30 p.m., Sunday noon to 4:00 p.m. Admission for adults
is $1; for children 8 to 12, 50 cents.
▲▲ **Delta County Historical Museum and Lighthouse**—Situated in **Ludington Park** on a finger of land
known as Sand Point, the museum is small but includes
lots of Indian and early settler artifacts, exhibits on
logging and nautical history and a room devoted to the
history of the Escanaba and Lake Superior Railroads,
established in 1881. The lighthouse is the restored top
from the Poverty Island Lighthouse. Open mid-May to
October 1, 1:00 to 9:00 p.m. A self-guided walk of almost
two miles past historical homes starts at the museum and
follows the lakefront.

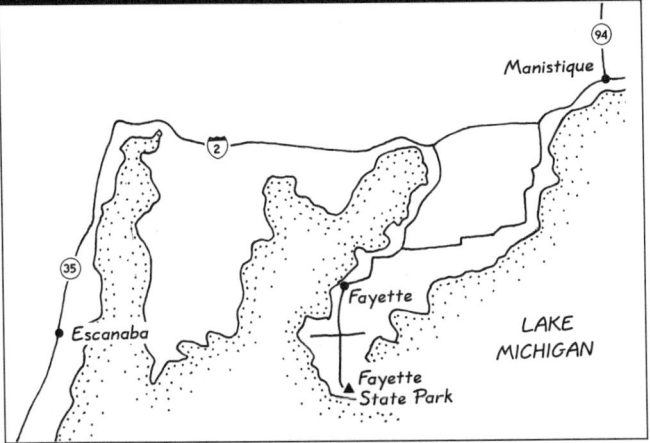

Escanaba—Fayette State Park—Manistique

▲▲▲ **Fayette State Park**—Some of the finest natural scenery in the Great Lakes is found in unique Fayette State Park, Garden, MI, (906) 644-2603, including a marvelous white sand beach, 90-foot-high limestone cliffs wrapped around a picturesque harbor, and hardwood forests surrounding a restored ghost town. On lovely Snail Shell Bay and harbor on the tip of the Garden Peninsula, the ghost town consists of more than 20 stone and wood buildings from the mid-1800s, when the town was a bustling iron smelting community. More than 500 people lived around the smelting enterprise by the 1880s. After the furnaces shut down in 1891, the town died.

An old blast furnace, charcoal kilns, lime kiln and quarry, blacksmith shop, opera house, company store, hotel, company office, homes of company supervisors, and warehouses can be seen in a short walking tour that includes the interpretive museum building. Also try some of the more than seven miles of well-marked hiking trails that loop through the 710-acre park, from deep in the woods to the edge of the cliffs. Park admission is $2 per car.

## Lodging

Don and Ruth Miller's **Garden Bay Motel** (906)
644-2258, in Cooks, has 200 feet of frontage and a swimming beach on Big Bay de Noc, midway down the Garden
Peninsula. Rates are $32 for a double housekeeping unit
($160 per week) and $25 for a single housekeeping
unit ($125 per week), with linens, dishes, cooking uten-
sils, and silverware.

## Camping

**Fayette State Park** contains 80 well-shaded campsites,
with boat camping in Snail Harbor on a first-come, first-
serve basis. Sand Bay Beach is just a short way from the
campground. **Portage Bay State Campgrounds**, 10
miles south of Garden, can be reached on SH 183 and the
very rough gravel Portage Bay Road. This campground
features 18 primitive campsites, each with a private path
to the lovely white sand beach. Portage Bay is strictly for
campers who want privacy.

## Food

The **Stonehouse**, 2223 Ludington Street, Escanaba, at
the junction of U.S. 2, U.S. 41, and SH 35, serves a full
lunch menu and prime rib and seafood dinners until
10:00 p.m., Monday through Saturday.

    **Rosies Place** on County Road 483 in tiny Garden is all
there is on the Garden Peninsula, but the menu covers
steak to Friday fish fry (perch and whitefish) specials,
salad bar on Friday night and Sunday, soups and snacks to
nachos. Open 7:30 a.m. to 9:30 p.m. seven days a week
year-round.

## Itinerary Options

For travelers with less time, from Escanaba there is a
much shorter route to Munising and Pictured Rocks
National Lakeshore Park. The quickest and most direct
way is Highways 2/41 through Gladstone to Rapid River,
then north on U.S. 41 and M-67 to Forest Lake (31 miles),
and east on M-94 eighteen miles to Munising. This

49-mile route takes only an hour and a half to Munising, which leaves time to check in and visit the National Park Service/U.S. Forest Service Information Center before boarding the Pictured Rocks boat cruise for a fabulous early evening cruise.

# MUNISING AND PICTURED ROCKS NATIONAL LAKESHORE

Raft over the biggest freshwater spring in Michigan before crossing the Upper Peninsula to Munising. See Pictured Rocks National Lakeshore's most beautiful waterfalls and stunning views from the cliffs before taking a late afternoon cruise along the colored cliffs.

## Suggested Schedule

| | |
|---|---|
| 7:30 a.m. | Check out and early breakfast. |
| 9:30 a.m. | Visit Kitch-iti-ki-pi. |
| 11:00 a.m. | Leave for Munising. |
| 12:30 p.m. | Lunch in Munising. |
| 1:30 p.m. | Stop in at the Hiawatha National Forest/ Pictured Rocks Lakeshore Information Center. |
| 2:00 p.m. | Drive to Munising Falls. |
| 4:50 p.m. | Board the Pictured Rocks Boat Cruise. |
| 9:00 p.m. | Dinner in Munising. |

**Travel Route: Fayette to Munising (80 miles)**
**Garden Peninsula to Kitch-iti-ki-pi:** Take U.S. 2 to Thompson, turn north on M-149 to CH 442, then left at Indian Lake State Park to CH 455, turn right past the West Shore Unit of Indian Lake State Park to M-149, the access to Palms Book State Park, with Kitch-iti-ki-pi (Big Spring) its major attraction. From U.S. 2, the drive to Kitch-iti-ki-pi is six miles.

    **Kitch-iti-ki-pi to Manistique and Munising:** From Kitch-iti-ki-pi and Indian Lake State Park, take CH 455 five miles east to Manistique. (If you return to U.S. 2 to Manistique, which is not necessary, five miles west of Manistique you'll come to Thompson State Fish Hatchery, worth a look at the process of raising the fingerlings that stock many of Michigan's streams and rivers.) Apart from seeing the Siphon Bridge, the only reason for driving to

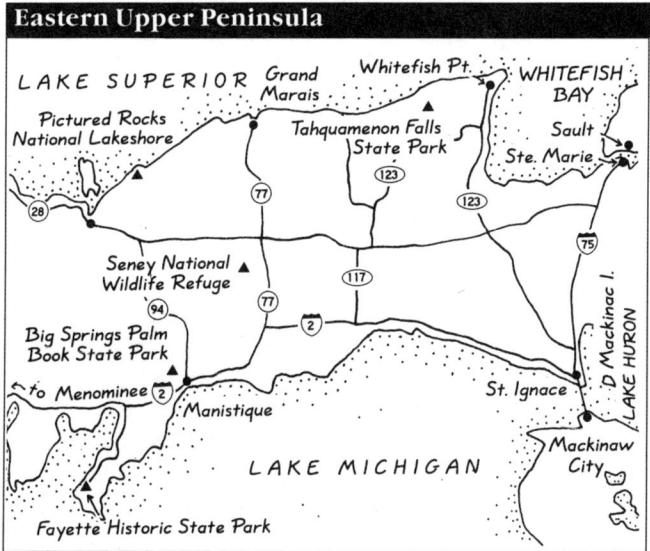

**Eastern Upper Peninsula**

Manistique is to get on paved M-94 to Munising. As an alternative, from M-149 and Indian Lake you can take a road directly north that turns into a gravel road south of Thunder Lake as it turns east and then north along Indian River.

**Lake Superior and Pictured Rocks National Lakeshore**

Lake Superior is the largest freshwater lake in the world. Canada's shoreline is far beyond the horizon, 160 miles away. On a calm sunny day, emerald green at the shoreline merges with deep blue as far as the eye can see. But on stormy days, waves capped with white foam lash furiously at cliffs, dunes, and wide sandy beaches.

Sediments deposited in shallow seas covering the park area millions of years ago were molded into their present forms by the last of four glaciers retreating about 10,000 years ago. A postglacial lake formed which was 40 feet higher than today's lake. Waves and frost carved stacks,

caves, arches, and promontories into the lakefront escarpment. Those formations have been given names such as
Grand Portal, Chapel Rock, Miners Castle, and Battleship
Row. Only about 2,000 years ago, Lake Superior settled to
its present level.

It's easy to understand why the Pictured Rocks coast
had great religious significance to Chippewa Indians who,
in 1836, ceded the eastern half of the Upper Peninsula to
the United States. Pictured Rock's forests were a hunting
ground for traders and trappers until, in 1867, these
woodlands began supplying hardwood charcoal for the
Schoolcraft Iron Furnace in Old Munising. Massive white
pine logging and periodic fires ensured bare land above
the rocks for the rest of the nineteenth century.

Tourism flourished in the nineteenth and early twen-
tieth centuries and, together with fishing fleets, kept
Munising and Grand Marais alive. Logging camps ceased
operation in 1952 and, on October 6, 1972, Pictured
Rocks National Lakeshore became part of the National
Park system.

Sandstone cliffs of 42-mile-long Pictured Rocks
National Lakeshore tower above Lake Superior, with
images painted on them by water and mineral seepage.
Inland streams channeling their way to the shore created
strange formations—caves, castles, and other shapes that
tantalize our imaginations. These streams flow over the
escarpments in delicate waterfalls.

The park is a mosaic of different natural systems that
can be glimpsed in a day or explored in a week or more.
You can view the colored rocks along Lake Superior from
the lake or cliffside viewing platforms, roam the wilderness in Beaver Basin over pine- and blueberry-covered
hills and through thick swamps, camp in the backcountry, listen to Lake Superior surf from the beaches, or hike
on parts of the nearby 43-mile Lakeshore Trail.

The three-mile-wide park has three distinct sections:
cliffs rising 50 to 200 feet painted pastels and carved by
nature into strange forms; Twelvemile Beach; and Grand
Sable Lake. This lake is cut off from Lake Superior by the

Grand Sable Banks, which rise to 275 feet in places and are topped by four square miles of shifting white sands— the Grand Sable Dunes—rising as much as 80 feet over the banks. The Lakeshore Trail across all of these sections can be accessed from mid-June to late September by a shuttle bus run by Alger County Public Transportation in Munising, (906) 387-4845.

**Sightseeing Highlights**
**▲▲ Palms Book State Park and Kitch-iti-ki-pi**— Michigan's largest spring-fed pond, Kitch-iti-ki-pi is about 300 feet long, 175 feet wide, and 40 feet deep. A short asphalt path leads from the parking area to a dock where you board a 30- to 40-passenger raft for a free 15-minute trip back and forth across the amazingly clear waters of Kitch-iti-ki-pi. Through two viewing boxes in the middle of the raft, you can see to the sand bottom, where 16- to 18-inch brown trout swim around and more than a dozen inlets pump more than 10,000 gallons of water a minute through churning sand into the pool. From Memorial Day through Labor Day, every day of the week from 9:00 a.m to 5:00 p.m., the raft is pulled from shore to shore by cable and pulley. (906) 341-2355.
**▲ Siphon Bridge**—The bridge over the Manistique River on M-94, three-fourths of a mile from Manistique, actually is four feet below the river's water level. Instead of a rail, the Siphon Bridge (a puzzling misnomer describing how the river speeds up as it flows under the bridge) has a cement fence and actually is part of a 3,000-foot-long concrete flume built in the early twentieth century by a paper mill to channel river water through the power plant. You can park near the brick water tower and walk across the bridge on the sidewalk for a stroll and a better view. The Manistique River has outstanding steelhead and salmon fishing.
**▲▲▲ The Hiawatha National Forest/Pictured Rocks National Lakeshore Visitor Information Center** in Munising will suggest areas that suit your interests, time, and capabilities. Follow M-28 to Cedar

Street, which intersects East Munising Avenue. The center
is on the corner, at 400 E. Munising Avenue. It is operated
jointly by the U.S. Forest Service and the National Park
Service.

Backpackers can obtain backcountry permits here. The
center also sells Forest Service Stamps and Golden Eagle
Passports and houses a Hiawatha Natural History Association bookstore and exhibits of the cultural and natural
history of the region.

Hours of operation are January 1 through March 31,
Tuesday through Saturday, 8:00 a.m. to 5:00 p.m.; April 1
through June 14, daily 9:00 a.m. to 5:00 p.m.; June 15
through September 15, daily 8:00 a.m. to 8:00 p.m.;
September 16 through December 31, daily 8:00 a.m. to
6:00 p.m. Telephone (906) 387-3700.

Hours at other park facilities are: **Munising Falls
Interpretive Center**, June 25 through September 4,
daily 10:00 a.m. to 4:00 p.m., (906) 387-4697 (also see
Sightseeing Highlights, below); **Grand Sable Visitor
Center**, year-round Monday through Friday, 8:00 a.m. to
4:30 p.m., (906) 494-2660 (see Day 12); and **Grand
Marais Maritime Museum and Ranger Station**, June
25 through September 4, daily 10:00 a.m. to 5:30 p.m.,
(906) 494-2669 (see Day 12).

▲▲ **Munising Falls**—Alger County boasts many scenic
waterfalls, eight of which are easily accessible: Laughing
Whitefish, Au Train, Wagner, Alger, Horseshoe, Munising,
Miners, and Grand Sable (see Day 12). Munising Falls,
the easiest falls to see in Alger County are east of Munising
on H-58, then north on Washington Street to an 800-foot
paved trail past an old charcoal furnace site deep into a
shaded canyon. Walk behind the 50-foot falls, in a hollow
carved by water, to view layers of sandstone cliff and
ferns, lichens, and moss covering wet rocky surfaces.
Stop at the Munising Falls Visitor Center to view exhibits
on the area's history. The National Park Service operates
an interpretive center at the falls which includes displays
on the geology, forest history, and blast furnace town that
occupied the site in the 1860s.

▲▲▲ **Pictured Rocks Cruise**—The Pictured Rocks Cliffs, which rise 200 feet from the lake and form the park's shoreline for 18 miles from Sand Point near Munising, must be seen from the water. The three-hour cruise passes pillars, arches, caves, and other unusual shapes that change color with the light. The afternoon cruises, with the sun shining directly on the rock, may be the best, but the morning light on the first cruise also is special. On the return leg of the trip, the captain brings the boat as close as possible to the cliffs. Pictured Rocks Cruise covers 37 miles round-trip, with as many as five boats out per day. The guides, especially Captain David Spencer, who sounds remarkably like radio announcer Paul Harvey, provide one of the better commentaries you'll hear on tour boats anywhere. From June 1 through June 30, two trips daily at 10:00 a.m. and 2:00 p.m.; July 1 through August 31, five trips daily at 9:00 and 11:00 a.m., and 1:00, 3:00, and 5:00 p.m. Rates are $14 for adults, $5 for children 6 to 12, and free for children 5 and under. Make reservations for the 5:00 p.m. cruise, when the setting sun produces wonderful color effects. Make reservations early, since cancellations of earlier cruises may crowd boats later in the day. (906) 387-2379.

### Lodging
The **Terrace Motel**, (906) 387-2735, Prospect Street, in Munising, two blocks off M-28, is in a quiet location, with a snowmobile track that starts just above the motel and is ideal for jogging. **Scotty's Motel**, (906) 387-2449, Cedar Street, is one block off M-28. **Sunset Resort Motel**, (906) 387-4574, is the only motel in town on Lake Superior. $50 per night double occupancy is standard for these motels.

### Camping
**Pictured Rocks National Lakeshore** has three campgrounds that are accessible by car: **Little Beaver Lake, Twelvemile Beach**, and **Hurricane River**. These campgrounds are available on a first-come, first-serve

basis. Little Beaver Lake in Beaver Basin, with a 5-mile
loop trail along Little Beaver and Big Beaver lakes, is near
the prettiest Lake Superior beach in the park, Chapel
Beach. Twelvemile Beach along a beautiful unbroken
stretch of beach is the best campground for direct access
to the lake and number of camping sites.

For the more adventuresome, experienced camper, the
park provides thirteen backcountry campgrounds with
3 to 10 sites every few miles over the 42.8 miles between
Munising Falls and Grand Sable. As in other parts of the
park, black flies, mosquitoes, and stable flies can be a real
nuisance in the summer, and insect repellent is essential.

Camping in the vicinity of Munising, within the
**Hiawatha National Forest**, includes the Bay Furnace,
Au Train Lake, Corner Lake, Pete's Lake, Widewaters,
Camp 7 Lake, and others. Contact the visitor information
center in Munising regarding national forest and national
lakeshore camping. Dick and Lynn Beckwith's **Buckhorn Otter Lake Campground**, (906) 387-4646,
located 1½ miles from the Buckhorn Restaurant, 2½
miles off M-94 and 7 miles off SH 13, is open all year and
has 72 good sites on Otter Lake, with hot showers and
other private campground facilities.

### Food
**Mr. B.'s Sandwich Shop**, (906) 387-3872, on M-28 in
Munising across from the Starlite Motel is a local favorite
for inexpensive and delicious Italian, Mexican, and Ameri-
can lunches and dinners, with homemade bread, spaghetti
sauce, even a pizza pasty. Open daily 6:00 a.m. to 11:00 p.m.
Big breakfasts, nightly seafood buffet, Saturday night
"Streak Fry" and Sunday brunch are specialties of
another local eatery, **Dogpatch**, located across from Mr.
B.'s Sandwich shop, open daily 6:00 a.m. to 11:00 p.m.

For a beautiful view of the lake (reserve a window
table), fine lake trout or whitefish dinners, Friday night's
all-you-can-eat fish fry, or Sunday brunch (10:00 a.m. to
2:00 p.m.), try the **Forest Inn Restaurant and Lounge**
(906) 387-4587, up the hill on M-28, two miles west of

Munising. This restaurant is open daily for lunch and dinner, 11:30 a.m. to 11:00 p.m.

**Itinerary Options**
Travelers who already have seen Pictured Rocks National Lakeshore, Tahquamenon Lake State Park, and Sault Ste. Marie may drive directly to St. Ignace from Fayette on U.S. 2. East on U.S. 2 from Naubinway to St. Ignace is one of the most beautiful drives on the Great Lakes. Wait until after the third week in May in order to enjoy springtime, but anytime between early May and late September, you will enjoy the combination of birches and evergreens, Epoufette Bay, and walks or jogs on Lake Michigan beaches. From Lake Superior State Forest you pass through Hiawatha National Forest. Stop at the Cut River Bridge, about 150 feet above the river, and walk to the middle of this long bridge or descend the stairs at the east end to the sandy beach. At Brevoort Lake there are two excellent campgrounds maintained by the U.S. Forest Service, about two miles apart, one on Lake Michigan and one off U.S.F.S. Road 3108 on the west end of the lake.

Indian Lake State Park offers campers a shallow lake that is better for walleye fishing than swimming. Indian Lake, Route 2, Box 2500, Manistique, MI 49854, (906) 341-2355, has two very different and widely separated lakeside camping areas: the newer West Shore Unit with 144 modern, thickly shaded sites and day-use facilities and, three miles away, the South Shore Unit, with 157 modern sites, a mile of sandy beach and better swimming, and no day-use facilities. Make your reservations at the less modern South Shore Unit. The Indian Museum in the park shows lore and artifacts of the first campers there, Ottawa, Ojibwa, and other tribes.

# MUNISING TO TAHQUAMENON FALLS STATE PARK

Take moderate walks to see a beautiful waterfall and cliff-side views from part of the park's 80-mile trail system. Take a scenic drive for a beach picnic on Twelvemile Beach in the park. Drive to the Grand Sable end of the park to see another waterfall and magnificent dunes. End the afternoon or the day in Grand Marais. (RVers and campers will head for Tahquamenon State Park and Muskallonge Lake State Park.)

## Suggested Schedule

| | |
|---|---|
| 7:30 a.m. | Breakfast. |
| 8:30 a.m. | Drive to Miners Falls and pick up a picnic lunch. |
| 10:30 a.m. | Chapel Beach area. |
| 12:00 noon | Picnic lunch at Twelvemile Beach. |
| 1:30 p.m. | Au Sable Light Station. |
| 2:00 p.m. | Log Slide view. |
| 2:30 p.m. | Grand Sable Visitor Center. |
| 3:00 p.m. | Sable Falls. |
| 3:30 p.m. | Grand Sable Dunes. |
| 4:30 p.m. | Maritime Museum in Grand Marais. |
| 5:00 p.m. | Dinner in Grand Marais, and check into lodgings. |
| 6:00 p.m. | If camping, drive to Tahquamenon Falls State Park. |
| 7:30 p.m. | Arrive at Tahquamenon Falls State Park. |

**Travel Route: Munising to Tahquamenon Falls State Park (132 miles)**
From Munising take H-58 for Miners area sightseeing, then return to the road east through Pictured Rocks for 55 miles through to Grand Marais. From Grand Marais, turn south on Highway 77 for 25 miles to Seney (unless you're planning to camp at Muskallonge Lake), left (east)

on Highway 28 to Highway 123, north on Highway 123 to
Newberry (27 miles), and continue another 25 miles to
Tahquamenon Falls State Park.

## Sightseeing Highlights

▲▲ **Miners Falls**—From the Visitor Information Center
on East Munising Avenue, continue north to H-58 and follow H-58 to Miners Castle Road, go four miles to the
Miners Falls turnoff on the right, then walk just over one
mile from the trailhead through sugar maple, yellow
birch, beech, and hemlock trees to the falls. The view
from the trail over Miners Basin toward Lake Superior is
spectacular. Miners Falls drops 60 feet through mist-filled
air over rocks painted with mineral stains.

▲ **Miners Area**—Castle-shaped cliffs, beach, river, falls,
and hiking trails are accessible by a 5-mile paved road
from H-58. The crumbling rocks of Miners Castle resemble castle turrets and are best viewed from the cruise
boat, but sandstone layers can be seen better from the
wooden platform along the cliff. Mile-long Miners Beach
Trail descends the escarpment in easy stages from the castle to the beach, revealing wonderful views of cliffs,
beach, and lake.

▲ **Chapel Beach, Chapel Rock, Grand Portal, and
Spray Falls**—Hikers can drive east from the Miners Area
on H-58 for eight miles to the Chapel parking area and
take the foot trail for a five-mile walk to see these scenic
areas or just a three-mile round-trip to see 90-foot
Chapel Falls.

The trail continues to Chapel Lake through a narrow
gorge, to Chapel Rock on the lake, lovely Chapel Beach,
then ascends the 200-foot cliffs to offer a view of spectacular Grand Portal and Indianhead Points. It continues to the
mouth of Mosquito River and returns to the parking lot.

▲ **The Beaver Basin area**—Three miles long and about
six miles wide, Beaver Basin is reached by Little Beaver
Road off H-58. This area is mainly for hikers and backcountry campers. After the Beaver Basin turnoff, H-58 is
unpaved and *very* rough gravel.

▲▲▲ **Twelvemile Beach Campground**—The road to this beach off H-58 goes through a spectacular birch forest that, especially on sunny days, is well worth the walk or drive. The beach ends at Hurricane River Campground to the east, at the beginning of Au Sable Point.

▲▲ **Au Sable Light Station**—Walk 1½ miles along the Lakeshore Trail to the recently restored Au Sable Light Station. Along the way visit a beach with the remains of ships wrecked on the Au Sable Reef. The lighthouse has been restored to its 1910 appearance.

▲▲▲ **Grand Sable Dunes**—Visit the Log Slide, a relic of the days when logs were chuted to Lake Superior, for a great view of Grand Sable Dunes and Grand Marais. The dunes extend about a mile between Grand Sable Lake, a popular boating and fishing lake, and Lake Superior. With more undisturbed open dunes on a freshwater lake than anywhere else in the world, Grand Sable Dunes is the third-largest dune system in Michigan. The dunes can be reached by a mostly level one-mile round-trip up steps and trails to the crests of dunes. The trail leads through jack pines full of orchids in summer. Five threatened plant species, including the calypso orchid, and 14 "special concern" species, such as the elegant dune grass and black hawthorn, are among the rare and protected plants within the dunes area.

▲▲ **Grand Sable Lake**—The lake has a bath house, and water skiing is permitted. The Light Station is a 4-mile walk round-trip from the lake.

▲▲ **Sable Falls**—From the Grand Sable Visitor Center, a foot trail leads to Sable Falls, reached from the parking area by a series of steps and a boardwalk down into the canyon of the roaring falls (.6 mile). From there the trail winds along Sable Creek to the rocky beach at Lake Superior. Grand Marais jetty is visible in the distance on the right, and Grand Sable Dunes rise on the left.

▲ **Maritime Museum**—Located on Coast Guard Point, about a mile beyond downtown Grand Marais, the museum displays photos of Coast Guard rescue activities, relics of Pictured Rocks shipwrecks, and other local

historic photos and maritime artifacts. From the Maritime
Museum along the promontory's coast back toward
Grand Marais is a wonderful beach for a long walk or a
swim for the hardy.

▲ **Seney National Wildlife Refuge**—Three miles
north of Germfask, on M-77 (turn at the Blaney Park corner) en route to Newberry, and 25 miles south of Grand
Marais, is the 95,500-acre Seney National Wildlife Refuge,
the largest east of the Mississippi. It was established in
1935 to protect bald eagles and other wildlife and to provide a protected stopover for Canada geese, snow geese,
and other migrating waterfowl and 230 other species of
birds. In early June, it's spring in the marsh, and lady's
slippers, starflowers, buttercups, and early summer wildflowers are starting to bloom. In mid-August, late summer
wildflowers are blooming, including hawkweeds, turtle-
heads, and butter-and-eggs. Fall is a beautiful time to
watch the changing seasons and migrating waterfowl.
There's a dike system to control the pools and marshes
which offers great bike rides in any season.

Seney's visitor center, (906) 586-9851, is open from
May 15 through September 30 and contains diorama
exhibits, films, and slide shows. Stop for a picnic or rest
en route from Grand Marais to Tahquamenon Falls. Take a
self-guided tour around the seven-mile Marshland Wildlife Drive (June 1 through October 31) and/or a 1½-mile
nature trail walk. A unique and more extensive guided
tour is available from June 15 until Labor Day. This two-
hour auto tour led by a park guide starts at 6:00 p.m. and
meanders through wetlands to view wildlife. Two- and
four-hour scenic canoe tours are available May to
October 15 from **Northern Outfitters**, Highway M-77,
Germfask, MI 49386, (906) 586-9801.

## Lodging
Grand Marais is a delightful place to stop over, especially
in a charming turn-of-the-century B&B. Bill and Bev
Madore's **Lakeview Inn of Grand Marais** on Highway
M-77, P.O. Box 297, Grand Marais, MI 49839, (906)

494-2612, is one of the oldest homes in town. Originally built in Seney in 1887, it was moved to Grand Marais in 1895. All five guest rooms, which share 3 baths, have period antiques. The rate is $55 double occupancy.

Several motels in Grand Marais, **Alverson's**, (906) 494-2681, across from the beach, and **Welker's Lodge**, (906) 494-2361, on the beach, have rooms for $55 double occupancy.

## Camping

Crowds flock to **Tahquamenon Falls State Park**, Paradise, MI 49768, (906) 492-3415, and its three campgrounds on summer weekends. Two of the campgrounds, River Bend and Overlook, with 183 sites (some shaded) and electrical facilities, are on bluffs overlooking the lower falls. Several miles away, the third campground, Rivermouth, has 76 modern sites and 60 rustic sites. Open year-round, the park is quiet and exceptionally beautiful in fall. Whether you're camping or hiking, bring plenty of insect repellent to deal with the hordes of blackflies. Michigan's second largest state park, Tahquamenon has more than 25 miles of foot trails. Especially popular is the 15-mile segment from the Lower Falls campground to Lake Superior.

If you don't have reservations at Tahquamenon Falls, consider staying at **Muskallonge Lake State Park** and heading for Tahquamenon Falls in the morning. On one side of the park is Lake Superior, and on the other is Muskallonge Lake. Between the two lakes are 179 modern campsites (most secluded are sites 151-179). There is heavy use from mid-July to mid-August, but spaces are still available. From Grand Marais, take County H-58 east to Muskallonge State Park. To reach Tahquamenon State Park from Muskallonge State Park, follow County H-37 (gravel) to Deer Park and south to Highway 123, then left (northeast) on Highway 123 to Tahquamenon (67 miles from park to park).

The **Newberry/Tahquamenon KOA**, 1/4 mile east of the intersection of M-28 and M-23, just before you enter

Newberry, is situated on a large wooded site. It features an indoor pool, sauna, whirlpool, and 120 campsites at $15 plus electricity.

## Food

**Welker's Lodge**, Canal Street on Coast Guard Point near the Maritime Museum, Grand Marais, has a restaurant with a complete menu for three meals. The **Sportsman Restaurant** in downtown Grand Marais only two short blocks from the Lakeview Inn serves whitefish dinners, Mexican food, and prime rib dinners. Both restaurants are open year-round seven days a week and serve until 10:00 p.m. Next to the Seney IGA in Seney, the friendly **Golden Grill** serves smorgasbord and other menu items year-round from 11:30 a.m. until 8:00 p.m.

# TAHQUAMENON FALLS TO SAULT
# STE. MARIE AND ST. IGNACE

In Whitefish Point, on beautiful Lake Superior, visit an outstanding marine history museum. Drive south to the state's oldest settlement, Sault Ste. Marie, which lies between Lake Superior and Lake Huron. Observation platforms, museums, and boat and train tours reveal to you how St. Marys' rapids become transformed into the largest and busiest lock system in the world. After a memorable dinner cruise through the locks, drive to St. Ignace, northern anchor of the Mackinac Bridge, eastern gateway to the Upper Peninsula, and departure port for tomorrow's Mackinac Island excursion.

## Suggested Schedule

| | |
|---|---|
| 7:30 a.m. | Breakfast. |
| 8:30 a.m. | View Lower Tahquamenon Falls. |
| 9:30 a.m. | Drive to Upper Tahquamenon Falls. |
| 11:00 a.m. | Drive to Great Lakes Shipwreck Museum at Whitefish Point. |
| 1:00 p.m. | Return to Paradise for lunch. |
| 1:45 p.m. | Drive to Sault Ste. Marie. |
| 3:00 p.m. | Soo Locks Visitors Center and Observation Platforms. |
| 4:00 p.m. | Tower of History. |
| 5:00 p.m. | Museum Ship Valley Camp. |
| 6:00 p.m. | Dinner cruise through Soo Locks. |
| 9:00 p.m. | Leave for St. Ignace. |
| 10:00 p.m. | Check in at St. Ignace. |
| 10:30 p.m. | Stroll to Father Marquette Memorial and around St. Ignace waterfront before bedtime. |

## Travel Route: Tahquamenon Falls to Sault Ste. Marie to St. Ignace (142 miles)

From Grand Marais, head south on M-77 to Seney, east on M-28 to M-123 north to Tahquamenon. Continue east on

M-123 to Paradise (16 miles), then make a side trip north
to **Whitefish Point** on beautiful **Whitefish Bay**, returning south on M-123 through Paradise to M-28, then east
on SH 28 to I-75 and north to Sault Ste. Marie. If you have
time, just before Sault Ste. Marie, make a left on M-221,
to 6 Mile Road in Brimley State Park, for a swim in the
warmest waters on Lake Superior. (The shaded, high-
numbered, modern campsites next to the lake are among
the best in the state.) Return on M-28 to I-75 into Sault
Ste. Marie. From I-75 take exit 392 and follow the Business Spur (Mackinaw Trail/Ashmun Street) about 3 miles
to Portage Avenue, turn right and go about a half mile to
Dock #2 or another half mile to Dock #1 for the Soo
Locks tours.

  After sightseeing around the Soo Locks, retrace your
route to I-75 south to U.S. 2, exit and drive about a half
mile east to Church Street, turn right on Church and go
three blocks to the entrance to Straits State Park. Otherwise, from I-75 follow the signs to downtown St. Ignace.

**Sightseeing Highlights**
**▲▲▲ The Falls at Tahquamenon Falls State Park**—
The largest of Michigan's more than 200 waterfalls and
the second-largest waterfall east of the Mississippi, Upper
Tahquamenon Falls cascades from a 200-foot-wide wall.
Four miles downstream, Lower Tahquamenon Falls
crashes no more than 20 feet over a series of rocks and
boulders in two sections around a tree-covered island. As
the Tahquamenon River flows through swamps, it picks
up a brown color, resulting in brownish water flowing
over the limestone cliffs of the falls and the series of
rocky steps at the upper and lower falls.

  For the best view of the lower falls, rent a rowboat at a
concession near the parking lot, row a few hundred yards
to the island, and then walk the trails circling the shoreline.
**▲▲ The Great Lakes Shipwreck Museum**—Located
on Whitefish Point north of Paradise, 20 miles from Tahquamenon Falls, the museum graphically portrays the
dangerous and unpredictable nature of Lake Superior,

from the wreck of the schooner *Invincible* in 1816 to the
wreck of the *Edmund Fitzgerald* in 1975. The museum
exhibits artifacts from dozens of wrecks, and stories of
the shipwrecks are shown on wide-screen video in
the theater. The museum is open seven days a week,
Memorial Day through October 15, 10:00 a.m. to 6:00 p.m.
Admission for adults is $2.50, for children 5-12 $1.50,
and children under 5 free.

▲▲ **Soo Locks Visitors Center and Observation
Platforms**—Long before white men came to the area,
Ojibwa Indians living nearby portaged their canoes
around the "Bawating" (rapids) of St. Mary's River to
reach Lake Superior. The Soo Locks began operation in
1855 with a single lock floating a ship around the rapids.
Today, an average of 30 times a day or 10,000 times a year,
the locks drop and rise 21 feet between Lake Huron and
Lake Superior, the water seeking its own level without the
aid of pumps. The new Poe lock is the largest lock in the
St. Lawrence Seaway and the only one that can handle
the superfreighters that are over 1,000 feet long and 105
feet wide.

There are several ways to watch the freighters move
through a series of four concrete, gated tubs. One of the
best is the Soo Locks Visitors Center and Observation
Platforms looking down at the McArthur Lock and over
the tops of the three other locks.

▲▲ **Tower of History**—The Tower of History stands 21
stories high between Dock #2 and the locks. You can't see
the locks very well, but the 20-mile-wide view of the
river and surrounding region is impressive. Admission is
$2.50 for adults, $1.50 for children 6 to 12. Open July 1
through August 31, 9:00 a.m. to 8:00 p.m.; May 15
through June 30 and September 1 through October 15,
10:00 a.m. to 5:00 p.m. For information, contact Le Sault
de Sainte Marie Historical Sites, P.O. Box 1668, Sault Ste.
Marie, MI 49783, (906) 632-3658.

▲▲ **Museum Ship Valley Camp**—Those who wonder
what it's like to live and work on one of the freighters that
ply the Great Lakes and pass through the Soo Canal can

visit the Museum Ship Valley Camp, part of the Port
Adventure complex around the boat and train departure
areas, gift shops, historic homes, and parks. In July and
August, the valley camp is open 9:00 a.m. to 9:00 p.m.
Between May 15 and June 30 and September 1 and
October 15, hours are 10:00 a.m. to 6:00 p.m. Admission
for adults is $4.50 and for children 6 to 12, $2.25. For
more information, contact Museum Ship Valley Camp, Le
Sault de Sainte Marie Historical Sites (address above).

▲▲ **Dinner Cruise through Soo Locks**—The best
way to see the locks is on a Welch Lock Tours' boat tour.
Several other cruises show you the two longest locks in
the world at the Soo Locks National Historic Site. The five
steel, double-deck tour boats on the American side of the
river leave one of the two docks every 20 minutes from
9:00 a.m. to 7:00 p.m. in July and August and on a reduced
schedule otherwise between May 15 and October 15. The
two-hour, 10-mile narrated tour costs $9 for adults and
$4 for children 6 to 15. A 3-hour buffet dinner cruise
combines the same 2-hour lock tour with a 1-hour cruise
on the St. Mary's River.

▲ **Soo Locks Train Tour**—A one-hour narrated train
tour leaves every half hour from 315-17 Portage Avenue
and follows the same route as the boats. It crosses the
International Bridge 175 feet above the locks to the Canadian lock, which offers an outstanding view of all the
locks, the river, and the rapids. The tour operates
Memorial Day to Labor Day, 9:00 a.m. to 5:30 p.m. Cost is
$3.25 for adults, $1.75 for children 6 to 12.

For more information, contact Soo Locks Tour Trains
and Twin Soo Tours, 315-17 W. Portage Avenue, Sault Ste.
Marie, MI 49783. Telephone (906) 635-5912. Another
source of information on area attractions is the Sault Area
Chamber of Commerce, 2581 I-75 Business Spur, Sault
Ste. Marie, MI 49783, (906) 632-3301.

## St. Ignace

At the southern tip of the Upper Peninsula, across the
Straits of Mackinac from Mackinaw City, St. Ignace is con-

nected to the lower peninsula by the Mackinac Bridge.
There are three ferry companies that serve St. Ignace,
Mackinaw City, and Mackinac Island (see Day 14). The St.
Ignace business district along the waterfront on State
Street, dominated by ferry landings and their parking lots,
offers much less gift and souvenir shopping and shorter
business hours than does downtown Mackinaw City.

## Lodging
Room rates generally are lower in St. Ignace than in Mackinaw City. Summer months can get very crowded, especially holidays and weekends, so try to call ahead for
room or campsite reservations. Most of St. Ignace's hotels
and restaurants are closed during the winter. **Aurora
Borealis Motor Inn**, 635 West U.S. 2, St. Ignace, MI
49781, (906) 643-7488, has 22 air-conditioned rooms, is
off the highway, three blocks from the ferry docks, and
has an adjacent restaurant. Rates are $52 to $58 in season.
**Dettman's Resort Motel**, 797 N. State Street, St. Ignace,
MI 49781, (906) 643-9882, is a waterfront resort of 77
units on 11 acres, with a private beach, pool, picnic and
barbecue area, badminton, volleyball, shuffleboard, and
a playground.

Open year-round, **Colonial House Inn** is a B&B and
motel, 90 North State Street, St. Ignace, MI 49781, (906)
643-6900, directly across the street from the ferry dock.
It offers shared bath units at the inn and private baths in
the motel. The innkeepers, a mother and daughter team,
live on the second floor of the inn. The building is called
the Chambers House and is a Registered National Historic
Home, once the residence of the John Chambers family,
which arrived from Ireland in 1846. Breakfast is served
daily from 7:30 to 9:00 a.m., and evening refreshments
are served from 6:30 to 7:30 p.m. Rates from May 15 to
October 1 are $48 to $65 per room double occupancy.
There is a special half-price rate for musicians who enter-
tain for an hour.

Instead of staying overnight in St. Ignace, consider parking your car there and taking a ferry to Mackinac Island to stay overnight on Days 13 and 14, leaving on Day 15. Staying on Mackinac Island is more pleasant and allows you to spend more time on the island. You may decide to splurge at **The Grand Hotel**, (906) 847-3331; the **Chippewa**, (906) 847-3341; the **Hotel Iroquois**, (906) 847-3321; or **Stonecliffe**, (906) 847-3355. Otherwise, room rates at Mackinac Island's tourist homes (see below) are as reasonable as those in St. Ignace or Mackinaw City.

The Grand Hotel, with per person doubles ranging from $120 to $225 with two meals, is ultra-luxury even for a small interior-view room. A guest room with balcony overlooking the Straits costs $360 for two with two meals. Tipping is not permitted, but 18 percent is added to the room rates. The Grand opened on July 10, 1887, and for more than a century the hotel has dominated the island as a famous landmark. With ample lawns and gardens and a highly visible location on the island's west bluff, the Grand's legendary opulence has been the backdrop for several Hollywood movies. The hotel promotes its historic connections; for example, the swimming pool is named the Esther Williams Grand Hotel pool.

The island has many "tourist homes"—restored residences that operate as inns or B&Bs and offer the best values: **Cloghaun Cottage**, (906) 847-3885, 7 rooms averaging $40; **Bogan Lane Inn**, (906) 847-3439, 4 rooms averaging $53; **The Inn on Mackinac**, (906) 847-3361, 44 rooms averaging $75; **Bayview Cottage**, (906) 847-3295, 7 rooms at $40 to $45; **LaChance**, (906) 847-3526, 18 rooms at $40 to $50; and **McNally Cottage**, (906) 847-3565, owned and operated by the same family for more than 100 years, with 8 comfortable units and rates of $35 to $60. **Hart's Haven**, (906) 847-3854, and **Small Point**, (906) 847-3758, are two are of the smallest tourist homes, with 5 and 6 rooms, respectively, renting at an average of $50. **Pine Cottage**, (906)

847-3820, with 13 cozy rooms in the village area, has rates from $39 to $60.

The **Metivier Inn**, Box 285, Mackinac Island, MI 49757, (906) 847-6234, or (616) 627-2055 in winter, with 17 rooms, is highly recommended as a splurge. On Market Street just east of City Hall, this inn was built in 1877 by Louis Metivier and recently renovated into a charming mix of British and French decor. Rooms with a queen-size bed and private bath range from $88 to $130 from July 1 through August 12. Efficiencies for up to 4 people rent for $145 to $160 from July 1 to August 12. Rates include a deluxe continental breakfast.

## Camping
**Straits State Park**, 720 Church Street, St. Ignace, MI 49781, (906) 643-8628, on a bluff overlooking Mackinac Bridge, has 313 modern campsites on 181 wooded and secluded acres. Lots 1-150 are closest to the beach (too rocky for comfortable swimming) and are the most private but are too small for large rigs. The largest, most secluded campsites are along the road marked "Bridge Overlook." The view of the bridge from the park is unsurpassed in St. Ignace. However, these "overflow" campsites are assigned only when the area campgrounds are full. Turnover in the park is high, so there's a good chance of getting a site even during the summer.

**Lakeshore Park**, 416 Pte. LaBarbe Road, St. Ignace, 49781, (906) 643-9522, a private campground 2½ miles west of the Mackinac Bridge on U.S. 2 (Exit 344B from I-75), has 75 sites with electricity on the Lake Michigan side of the highway. Twenty-five have sewer hookups. Sites cost $11 plus electricity. This campground will take you by van to the boat dock in St. Ignace. The nearby **KOA St. Ignace**, (616) 436-5643, on U.S. 2, has twice as many sites for $17 each plus electricity.

## Food
Several restaurants on Portage Street in Sault Ste. Marie serve lunch and dinner year-round. Try **The Antlers**,

804 E. Portage, for burgers and seafood; **Cafe du Voyageur**, 205 W. Portage, just a block from the Soo Locks, serves excellent soups and salads. Both are open daily from from 11:00 a.m. to 10:00 p.m. Watch the locks while dining at **Lockview Restaurant**, where the daily specialty from 5:00 to 10:00 p.m. is whitefish.

**The Galley**, 241 State Street, St. Ignace, (906) 643-7960, a family-style restaurant open seven days, 7:00 a.m to 10:00 p.m. from mid-May through mid-October, serves whitefish and lake trout caught fresh daily in Lakes Huron and Superior. Their extensive fish, chicken, and beef menu includes entrées at $5.95 to $16.95. **Northern Lights Restaurant**, 645 West U.S. 2, serves breakfast, lunch, and dinner from 7:00 a.m. to 10:00 p.m., but their breakfast for under $3 is your best bet.

### Itinerary Option: Excursions in Canada

Directly across St. Mary's River, Sault Ste. Marie in Ontario, Canada, is worth a side trip. Stroll through **Bellevie Park** along the waterfront; and tour the M.S. *Norgoma*, at the Norgoma dock, at Foster Drive, (705) 942-6984, the last of the overnight passenger cruise ships built on the Great Lakes. Guided tours start every half hour. Take a two-hour narrated tour of the city from a double-decker bus departing from the Algoma Central Railway Station at Bay and Dennis streets. (705) 759-6200. Fares are adults $7, children 5 to 17 $3.50, and families $16.50. If you have even more time, consider a one-day trip by train to **Agawa Canyon**, (705) 632-8201, from Sault Ste. Marie, Ontario, especially in the fall season. The train leaves at 8:00 a.m., arrives at Agawa Canyon (114 miles) at 11:30 a.m., and returns to Sault Ste. Marie by 5:00 p.m. Tickets cost $36 for adults, $13 to $17.50 for children, depending on the season, and $6 for children under 5.

## MACKINAC ISLAND

Tiny Mackinac Island, with lots of tourists and no cars, packs in more natural and historic sightseeing, more outdoor recreation and shopping than any other place in the Great Lakes. Take the ferry from St. Ignace, rent a bicycle, and pedal around the state park, visit the old fort, other historic buildings, and the Grand Hotel, tootle through tearooms and souvenir shops, and deal in your own way with Mackinac Island fudge and ice cream. Anyone with an excuse to splurge should dine or stay at the Grand Hotel.

### Suggested Itinerary

| | |
|---|---|
| 8:00 a.m. | Boat to Mackinac Island. |
| 8:30 a.m. | Breakfast on the island. |
| 9:15 a.m. | Visitor Center and walking tour of town. |
| 11:00 a.m. | Rent bicycle to tour Mackinac Island State Park or take carriage tour. |
| 1:00 p.m. | Lunch or picnic lunch. |
| 2:00 p.m. | Continue bicycle tour and/or visit Fort Mackinac. |
| 5:30 p.m. | Dinner at Grand Hotel or other island restaurant. |
| 7:30 p.m. | After-dinner stroll in town. |
| 8:00 p.m. | Ferry back to St. Ignace. |

### Mackinac Island

Mackinac Island can be reached by ferry, airplane, or private boat. Three ferry companies operate frequent daily service from Mackinaw City and St. Ignace. Round-trip fares are $9 for adults, $5.75 for children 5 to 12, free for children under 5, and $3 per bike. **Arnold Mackinac Island Ferry**, dock phone (906) 847-3351 or 643-8275, the oldest of the three ferry lines with maritime history going back to 1878, leaves from St. Ignace's docks on State Street. All-day parking is free. From June 17 to

September 3, there are 23 departures from St. Ignace
daily between 7:30 a.m. and 10:00 p.m. In early spring
and late fall, there are only six crossings daily. The ride
takes about 25 minutes. Also operating from St. Ignace
and Mackinaw City, **Shepler's Mackinac Island Ferry**,
(616) 436-5023, has a frequent schedule—every half hour
to every 15 minutes in season. (Shepler's also has a car
care center, where you can have your vehicle refueled
and its oil changed while you tour Mackinac Island.) **Star
Line Mackinac Island Passenger** Service, 590 N. State
Street, St. Ignace, (906) 643-7635, is the third ferry
company.

Once you're off the ferry, rent a bicycle to get around
this 3- by 2-mile island. The town is situated at the edge
of a hilly forest threaded with bicycle paths and cut by
ravines. The island's rim is encircled by a flat and fre-
quently crowded bike and walking route (M-185). On
Huron Street, the main street, sparkling white buildings
full of character are filled with shops that seem to have
one thing in common: selling delicious chocolate fudge.
Across from Father Marquette's statue in Marquette Park is
the **State Park Visitor Center**. Stop there for a map and
information about the island.

Your self-guided walking tour of the fort and the hotel,
which overlook the town from high on bluffs, starts right
at the boat docks. Fort Street leads up the hill to **Fort
Mackinac**, its 14 buildings dating from 1780 to 1885.
Costumed guides conduct tours on the hour. The
Officers' Stone Quarters is the oldest stone building in
the state. The buildings are furnished in nineteenth-
century style and offer historic displays and dioramas.
During the day there are regular demonstrations of cannon and musketry. Fort Street also leads to Market Street
and the **American Fur Company Store**, which honors
the remarkable medical pioneer Dr. William Beaumont,
fort surgeon in the 1820s and 1830s; the **American Fur
Company Trading Center**, with a museum of the Mackinac fur trade (open June to mid-September, Monday
through Saturday 11:00 a.m. to 5:00 p.m., Sunday 1:00 to

5:00 p.m.); **Biddle House**, oldest house on the island;
and **Benjamin Blacksmith Shop**, a working replica of
an 1880s blacksmith shop. Admission to all of these
historical sites and buildings is $5 for adults, $2.50 for
children ages 6 to 12, and $15 for families.

Turn right at Cadotte Street to ascend to the **Grand
Hotel**, just blocks from the ferry dock. Originally built
by the railroads to accommodate train passengers who
would take the ferry to the island from Mackinaw City,
the completely remodeled 286-room hotel boasts the
title of "world's longest" at 880 feet. A magnificent white
structure on 500 acres of grounds, the Grand charges $5
until 6:00 p.m. just to walk into the hotel to gawk at the
lobby, the guests, and the famous porch stretching the
length of the hotel. The dining room is open to the public, as is the Terrace Room for dancing. Both have a strict
dress code: ties and jackets for men and dresses for
women.

**Mackinac Island State Park** includes geological formations like Arch Rock and Sugar Loaf and breathtaking
vistas of the straits. Eighty percent of the island is part of
the state park. There is no admission charge. The route
around the shore is about 8 miles and can get crowded
on holidays and weekends, but otherwise it is a very scenic and pleasant bicycle ride, with many small rocky
beaches for resting or a picnic. Above the shore, you can
bicycle behind Fort Mackinac to Arch Rock Bicycle Trail,
then along Leslie Avenue to Scott's Road around the
northern tip of the island down to British Landing for
refreshments at concession stands. For a somewhat
shorter and less hilly ride, turn left off Leslie Avenue on
Bicycle Trail to Rifle Range Road, Garrison Road, and British Landing Road to British Landing. Then return to town
by turning south (left) on Lake Shore Road (M-185).

Another much shorter ride or hike is out Cadotte Avenue to Annex Road, past a number of magnificent Victorian summer homes. Take the Stonecliffe Road fork to
the left instead of continuing on Annex Road and head
for **Stonecliffe Mansion**. Built in 1924, and located on a

bluff with a good view of the straits, it is a fine example of German Tudor architecture. From the Stonecliffe Shore Road behind the property, you can hike on the Norton Trail running north along the coast and connecting with the Packard Trail and the Tranquil Bluff Trail, which heads back to town.

Bicycle liveries are located throughout downtown on Huron Street and at selected hotels. Bike rental companies provide a selection of 3-, 5-, or 10-speed bikes, including all-terrain. Child carriers also are available. Check out Iroquois Bikes, (906) 847-3221, next to Shepler's Ferry; Island Bicycle Livery, (906) 847-3372; Lakeside Bikes, (906) 847-3351; Mission Point Bikes, (906) 847-3312, for fat tire bikes; or Ryba's Bikes, (906) 847-6261.

There are more than 500 horses on the island during tourist season. **Mackinac Island Carriage Tours**, a consortium of 30 local families, uses about 300 of these horses to transport passengers in two- or three-horse carriages past the Grand Hotel up to Surrey Hill. Here passengers transfer to a three-horse carriage for the trip across the island to Arch Rock, then to Fort Mackinac.

An alternative is to rent your own "surrey with a fringe on top" or a "ride yourself" horse on an hourly basis. Several companies operate rentals of horses for saddle riders and "drive yourself" carriages, taxis, and carriage rides: Arrowhead Carriages, (906) 847-6112; Carriage Tours Livery, (906) 847-6152; Carriage Tours Taxi, (906) 847-3323; Carriage Tours Tickets, (906) 847-3325; Chambers Riding Stable, (906) 847-6231; Cindy's Riding Stable, (906) 847-3572; Gough Livery, (906) 847-3435; and Jack's Livery Stable, (906) 847-3391.

**Food**
**Little Bob's** on Astor Street, (906) 847-3512, claims to serve "the bestest food on the island," which comes close to the truth. The dinner buffet for $11.95 is really a feast including salad, soup, hot entrées like ribs, chicken, and fish, hot vegetable side dishes, potatoes and a rice selection, plus fresh bread and tempting desserts, including

bread pudding, strawberry shortcake, pies, and several varieties of muffins. Little Bob's serves breakfast, lunch, and a selection of dinner dishes for those who prefer to pass on the buffet.

**Murray's Delicatessen** at the Murray Hotel on Main Street, (906) 847-DELI, has 50 sandwich selections with clever names like "Fowl Weather" (chicken salad), "Ernest Hamingway" (ham), and "Rye Rye Blackbird" (turkey on grilled rye). All sandwiches have generous portions and can be ordered for carry-out. Murray's also serves soups, pizza, breakfast items, fudge, desserts, frozen yogurt, and so on. **The Village Inn** on Hoban Street, (906) 847-3542, is one of the few restaurants on the island with an outdoor deck. The inn serves lunch, dinner, and late-night menus. Sandwiches and salads are excellent and reasonably priced. Vegetarians and light eaters have lots of choices. Two people can lunch for under $10.

Mackinac Island is the fudge center of the Great North (and perhaps the universe). Fudge shops line Huron Street, competing with "horse fudge" for visitors' attention. My favorites are rich and smooth Kilwin's and Ryba's: **Kilwin's Candy Kitchen** with two locations on Huron Street, one of which serves Haagen-Dazs ice cream (which is strange since Kilwin's own ice cream is better); and **Ryba's Fudge Shops** with 11 flavors, the island's only year-round fudge shop, cited for lifting local spirits through long winters.

## DAY 15

## ST. IGNACE TO LITTLE TRAVERSE BAY AREA

The frontier environment is re-created at Fort Michilimackinac and its houses, barracks, and church in Colonial Michilimackinac State Park. After visiting the park and its maritime and other museums, drive the beautiful M-119 via Cross Village around to Harbor Springs on Little Traverse Bay and continue to Petoskey and Charlevoix.

### Suggested Itinerary

| | |
|---|---|
| 8:30 a.m. | Check-out and breakfast in St. Ignace or Mackinaw City. |
| 9:00 a.m. | Visit Colonial Michilimackinac State Park, Fort Michilimackinac and Mackinac Maritime Museum. |
| 11:30 a.m. | Leisurely drive to Harbor Springs on M-119. |
| 1:00 p.m. | Lunch in Harbor Springs. |
| 2:00 p.m. | Visit Harbor Springs and Petoskey State Park. |
| 5:00 p.m. | Stroll through Petoskey's Gaslight District. |
| 7:30 p.m. | Dinner in Ellsworth. |
| 9:30 p.m. | Relaxing evening in the Little Traverse Bay area. |

**Travel Route: St. Ignace to Ellsworth (93 miles)**
Drive on C-81, and then take U.S. 31 south to Carp Lake Village. Go west on Gill Road through Bliss, taking a right to Sturgeon Bay en route to Cross Village, entrance to the magical M-119 scenic drive—a tunnel of trees to Harbor Springs. Stay on M-119 through Harbor Springs to U.S. 31 to Petoskey State Park and Petoskey. Continue another 16 miles south as far as Charlevoix and possibly Fisherman's Island State Park, just a few miles south of Charlevoix. Those lodging or dining in Ellsworth should take C-65 from Charlevoix and take a left on C-48 into Ellsworth (7 miles).

**Sightseeing Highlights**

▲▲▲ **Mackinac Bridge**—The world's longest suspension bridge (26,444 feet), Mackinac Bridge is known as "Mighty Mac," the bridge that couldn't be built. A bridge across the straits was first proposed in 1884, but it wasn't until November 1, 1957, that Michigan's Upper and Lower Peninsulas were spanned. Walking across the bridge, a famous annual event, is permitted only on Labor Day. The toll for cars is $1.50; with a one-axle trailer, $2.50; and with a two-axle trailer, $3.50.

▲▲ **Colonial Michilimackinac State Park**—At the southern end of the bridge (I-75, Exit 339) is the park, which consists of a restoration of the original French and British fort. There's also the Mackinac Maritime Museum in the restored Old Mackinac Point Lighthouse and Mackinac Marine Park, with Great Lakes memorabilia, old vessels, and Straits of Mackinac nautical history. Three miles southeast on U.S. 23 to Cheboygan is Old Mill Creek State Park with a museum, sawmill, craft demonstrations, nature trails, archaeological excavations, and other interpretive programs. Admission for all these places is available in a combined ticket: $9 for adults, $5 for children 6 to 12. Open May 15 to June 15, 9:00 a.m. to 5:00 p.m.; mid-June to Labor Day, 9:00 a.m. to 7:00 p.m.; and after Labor Day to mid-October, 10:00 a.m. to 4:00 p.m.

▲▲▲ **Harbor Springs**—Shops, galleries, yachts, and sailboats are nothing less than smart in this town; the sidewalk cafes are full of pretty people who've partied often and late. The town's 19 historic buildings are delightful to look at, but so are the rest of the painted and primed summer homes. Everyone looks bright, preppy, and peppy. Harbor Point's name families are guarded and literally inaccessible except to approved visitors—and it's all thoroughly enjoyable on a summer's day.

▲▲▲ **Petoskey's Gaslight District**—Starting at the intersection of Lake Street and Howard Street, bounded by Petoskey Street and Park Avenue, and bordered by Pennsylvania Park, Petoskey's Gaslight District of 1800s building facades provides one of the most picturesque

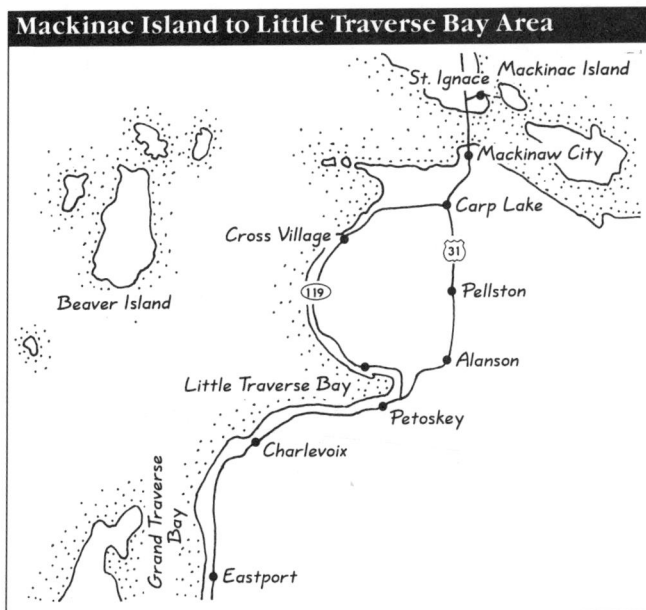

**Mackinac Island to Little Traverse Bay Area**

shopping areas in the Great Lakes. More than 70 retail stores are in this six-block area.

▲▲▲ **Charlevoix**—Another very pretty resort town between Lake Michigan and Lake Charlevoix, Charlevoix itself has few specific sightseeing attractions. Beaver Island offshore is a wonderful place for bicycling. The area also has four delightful beaches. Lake Michigan Beach is just south of the pier, a short walk from downtown along Park Avenue or along Pine River Channel on the new south shore walkway. Mount McSauba is a primitive, natural beach on Lake Michigan, with no lifeguards or other facilities. Behind the dunes is a series of well-kept trails through a beautiful wooded area. Depot Beach on Lake Charlevoix has warmer water and calmer waves than Lake Michigan; and Fisherman's Island State Park has seven miles of Lake Michigan beach. (See Camping, below.)

## Lodging

**Charlevoix Country Inn**, 106 West Dixon Avenue, Charlevoix, MI 49720, (616) 547-5134, has nine guest rooms and two suites with full kitchens and private baths. Most rooms have a view of Lake Michigan. Rates include breakfast and a wine and cheese sampling in the afternoons. Each guest receives a welcome basket with local products such as preserves and candies. Hot beverages, juice, and a newspaper are delivered to guests' doors prior to breakfast. Open from May through October. Rates range from $65 to $150 per night.

   **The Patchwork Parlor B&B**, 109 Petoskey Avenue, U.S. 31 N., Charlevoix, MI 49720, (616) 547-5788, is only a few doors from the Lake Michigan beach and an easy walk to downtown and the harbor. All guest rooms at the Patchwork have private baths. Rates ($48 double) include complimentary breakfast.

   Julie and Buster Arnim's **House on the Hill**, 206 Lake Street, Ellsworth, Michigan 49729, (616) 588-6304, is a beautifully remodeled Victorian farmhouse on 53 acres overlooking St. Clair Lake. Three wonderful guest rooms are priced $65 double including a full breakfast, with shared bath.

## Camping

**Petoskey State Park**, 2475 Harbor-Petoskey Road, Petoskey, MI 49770, (616) 347-2311, arcs for a mile around Little Traverse Bay. Petoskey is one of the best lakefront state parks anywhere for camping, swimming, sunbathing, beachcombing, and jogging. The two campgrounds have 190 modern sites with electrical hookups and good access to showers and washrooms. The older campsites are outstanding—wooded, secluded, and a short walk over dunes to the beach. Sites numbered 91-190 are newer, have paved slips, and are more accessible for RVs. North and south of the park are the shopping areas and restaurants of Harbor Springs (3 miles) and Petoskey. During the summer, the park has live concerts on Friday at 12:15 p.m. and Tuesday at 12:15 p.m. and 7:00 p.m.

**Fisherman's Island State Park**, P.O. Box 456, Charlevoix, MI 49720, (616) 547-6641, may be the best kept secret among Michigan's state parks, but it isn't for everyone. Its 2,000 acres of unspoiled wilderness contain 90 beautiful sites that are lightly used even in summer's peak. There are no services and no electricity. Bring everything. A 2-mile dirt, potholed road runs along Lake Michigan. Park in the small parking area near the entrance, walk to find a site, and check the road before driving it. You'll love it or leave it. From Charlevoix, drive 5 miles on U.S. 31 to Bell's Bay Road, turn right (west), and drive for 2 ½ miles to the park.

**Young State Park**, Box 3651, Boyne City, MI 49712, (616) 582-7523, has three modern campgrounds with 294 sites, electricity, and showers. The best sites are along a marvelous Lake Charlevoix beach in the Terrace and Oak units. The newer Spruce campground has little shade or privacy. From Petoskey take Highway 31 to Walloon Lake and Highway 75 to Boyne City. Drive 2 ½ miles north on County 56 to the park.

**Food**

For a light lunch in Harbor Springs, take your pick of two different, excellent places. **Juilleret's**, 130 State Street, (616) 626-2821, near the harbor, is a family restaurant with reasonable prices. **Turkey's Too**, 250 E. Main Street, (616) 347-3956, is a casual restaurant serving pizza, calzone, and a selection of sandwiches. The menu includes a vegetarian sandwich for $2.90 and a heart smart pizza (oat bran crust with vegetable toppings and low-fat mozzarella) as well as more conventional choices. Open every day 4:30 to 10:00 p.m. and 4:30 to 11:00 p.m. during the summer and on weekends during the rest of the year.

Stay at a campground near Ellsworth and then splurge on an unforgettable gourmet dinner at **The Rowe** or **Tapawingo**. The Rowe, (616) 588-7351, on Lake Street just a short drive from the House on the Hill, has been serving gourmet meals in Ellsworth for 17 years. The sign over the bar reads "Bacchus opens the gate of the heart," and The Rowe maintains a wine cellar sure to delight wine lovers and open the heart. A changing selection of wines (champagnes, California, Michigan, French, Italian, German, New Zealand, Australian) by the glass costs $4.50 to $10 and by the bottle from $12. Retail sale wine is also available. The menu changes daily, and entrées include soup, salad, and appetizer. Entrées are $17 to $30 and usually include a vegetarian selection as well as seafood, beef or veal, and pork. Desserts are $2 to $8. Open seven nights a week.

Tapawingo, 9502 Lake Street, in Ellsworth (616-588-7971), was opened by a former chef from The Rowe. In a lovely, homey setting, with a spacious yet intimate dining room, entrées range from $22 to $32 and include appetizer and soup or salad. The menu changes daily and may include items like grilled tuna with salsa, veal with Roquefort sauce, rack of lamb with lentils, and whitefish with spiced pecans. An extensive wine selection is available by the glass at $4 to $8 or by the bottle at $14. Open seven nights a week.

# GRAND TRAVERSE REGION AND LEELANAU PENINSULA

The Grand Traverse region has beautiful lakes such as Walloon, the fingers of Charlevoix, long Torch Lake, tiny gem Clam Lake, and many others. In spring, Old Mission Peninsula is filled with the sweet scent of cherry orchards in bloom. Leelanau's prim and pretty coastal towns, hidden lakes, and hilly back roads invite you to linger. Wineries improbably thrive in the frosty northland; towns are thick with galleries and shops. At the hub of it all is the cherry capital of Michigan, Traverse City.

## Suggested Schedule

| | |
|---|---|
| 8:00 a.m. | Breakfast and check out. |
| 9:00 a.m. | Drive up Old Mission Peninsula. |
| 12:00 noon | Lunch in Traverse City and sight-see in Traverse City and on Old Mission Peninsula. |
| 3:00 p.m. | Leelanau Peninsula and Leland. |
| 6:30 p.m. | Dinner in Leland. |
| 8:00 p.m. | Sunset stroll through Fishtown. |

**Travel Route: Charlevoix to Leland (175 miles)**

From Charlevoix, Ellsworth, or Little Traverse Bay, it's about 60 miles directly to Traverse City and 75 miles on the suggested scenic route. Take U.S. 31, the Old Dixie Highway from Norwood south. Drive on C-593 on the east shore of Torch Lake past Clam Lake near the Grass River Natural Area, then on M-72 through Williamsburg to Acme past the Grand Traverse Resort and into Traverse City. Drive up Old Mission Peninsula, a 40-mile round-trip, up Peninsula Drive along the West Bay and down Bluff Road along East Bay. Head for Leelanau Peninsula up M-22. It's 36 miles to the tip at Leelanau State Park, driving through Northport. Head down the west coast of the peninsula through Christmas Cove on M-22 to

Leland, visiting wineries along the way. With side trips to
wineries, it's about 20 miles of driving.

**Traverse City**
The best time to be in Traverse City is during the
**National Cherry Festival**, the second week in July, for
three parades on Front Street, nightly concerts in the
Open Space by Clinch Park, concerts by the Traverse
Symphony Orchestra, and plays at the Cherry County
Playhouse.

**Sightseeing Highlights**
▲▲▲ **Old Mission Peninsula**—More than a half century after the first settlement, a Presbyterian mission, a
farmer planting tart red cherries unwittingly filled the
economic gap left by departing lumberjacks. Drive
through Old Mission Peninsula, 18 miles long and 1½
miles wide, in spring when the cherry blossoms are in
full bloom or in the fall when the leaves are changing
color. Visit the Chateau Grand Traverse winery, 7½ miles
north of Traverse City on Center Road (M-37) for taste
tests of merlot, riesling, and pinot noir and superb views
of Grand Traverse Bay and Power Island. Drive 2½ miles
farther north for the **Bowers Harbor Inn**, one of the
nicest places to watch the sunset through the pines and
oaks, perhaps before enjoying the inn's haute cuisine (see
Food, below).
▲▲▲ **Leelanau Peninsula**—Follow M-22 north on
Leelanau Peninsula to the towns of Suttons Bay, Northport, and, around the west side, Leland, with side trips to
the Grand Traverse Lighthouse at the tip and scenic
Christmas Cove and Peterson Park on the way south. In
Suttons Bay at the Painted Bird, in Omena at the Tama-
rack Craftsmen Gallery, and in Northport at the Art Gallery and Joppich's Bay Street Gallery, a total of more than
100 local artists and craftspeople exhibit their work.
▲ **Leelanau Vineyard Touring**—You have a choice of
four vineyards on the peninsula, open May 1 through
October 31. Leelanau Ltd. is near Omena (616) 946-1653,

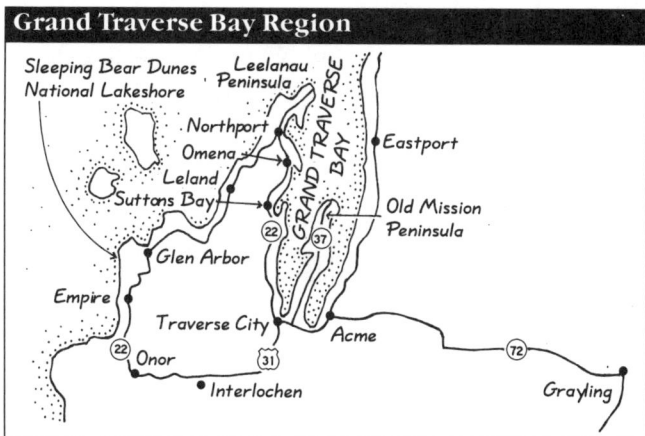

**Grand Traverse Bay Region**

11:00 a.m. to 6:00 p.m. Monday through Saturday, and 12:00 noon to 6:00 p.m. Sunday. The other three are clustered around Leland: Good View Vineyards, (616) 256-7165, adjacent to the Manitou Farm Market, 11:00 a.m. to 6:00 p.m. Monday through Saturday, and 12:00 noon to 6:00 p.m. Sunday; Boskydel Vineyard, (616) 256-7272, on the east side of Lake Leelanau along C-641, 11:00 a.m. to 6:00 p.m. Monday through Saturday, and 12:00 noon to 6:00 p.m. Sunday; and L. Mawby Vineyards, (616) 271-3622, 1:00 to 6:00 p.m. Thursday through Saturday.

▲▲▲ **Leland**—This picturesque town sits between Lake Michigan and Lake Leelanau. There's a short stretch of river between the two and a double row of shanties that date back to the 1800s—Fishtown—where you can buy souvenirs, eat, and watch marina activities. Park in one of the three public parking lots (River Street east of First Street, First Street between Park and Bill streets, or Pine and Cedar adjacent to the historical museum and library) and walk through downtown shops and Fishtown.

**Lodging**
**Northport**, on Leelanau Peninsula, 30 miles north of Traverse City and 8 miles south of the tip of the "Little

Finger" of Michigan, has three of northwest Michigan's
nicest B&Bs. At **Apple Beach Inn**, 617 M-22, Box 2,
Northport, MI 49670, (616) 386-5022, guest rooms are
comfortably furnished with lovely antiques. Guests enjoy
lemonade served in the beach gazebo, afternoon tea or
sherry, chocolates at bedside, home-baked muffins with
gourmet coffees in the morning, and other niceties that
make this a very special place. Rates are $65 double with
private baths. Barbara McCann's **Mapletree Inn**, Route 1
Box 169, Northport, MI 49670, (616) 386-5260, is nestled
on two acres with a pond and a cherry orchard. A two-
room suite accommodates up to six. Rates are $65
double. **Old Mill Pond Inn**, 202 East Third Street,
Northport, MI, (616) 386-7341, on a bluff overlooking the
Old Mill Pond, is only three blocks from downtown. Five
guest rooms share three full baths. Open year-round.
Two-night minimum stay on some holiday weekends.
Rates range from $55 to $70.

**Camping**
Norm and Doris Nevinger's small private campground,
**Old Mission Inn Campsites**, has 29 sites on Old
Mission Peninsula. The address is 18599 Old Mission
Road, Traverse City, MI 49684, (616) 223-7770. Drive 18
miles north of Traverse City on M-37, 1½ miles east on
Old Mission Road. The swimming there is great, and
cherry picking is offered in season. The rate is $14, plus
$2 for electricity.
   On Leelanau Peninsula, there's another good private
campground for RVs and tent camping. You'll enjoy Don
and Anita Novak's **Leelanau Pines Campground**, Route
1, Cedar, MI 49621, (616) 228-5742, on beautiful Lake Leelanau. Take M-72 west to CR 651, turn right to go through
Cedar and right again on CR 645, go ½ mile to CR 643,
then turn right and drive almost 4 miles to the campground. The rate is $15, plus hookup charges.
   **Leelanau State Park**, Route #1, Box 49, Northport, MI
49670, (616) 386-5422, has only 47 rustic sites in a grove
of pine and cedar on a beautiful shoreline adjacent to a

historic lighthouse. All have privacy, but campsites 26 through 35 and 39 are the best. The park is eight miles north of Northport on CR629. I highly recommend making reservations here.

You can make **Interlochen State Park**, Interlochen, MI 49643, (616) 276-9511, your base for trips to Traverse City, Leelanau, Sleeping Bear National Lakeshore, and the whole Grand Traverse area. The park is 14 miles southwest of Traverse City on U.S. 31 and 1½ miles south on M-137. Of the 550 sites, 478 have electrical hookups and access to showers. The largest sites are lots 11 through 47 on the north loop and lots 304 through 348 on the south loop. A sandy beach on Duck Lake, boat rentals, and thick woods, including stands of 300-year-old virgin white pine, compensate for crowded sites. Across M-137 is a 72-site rustic campground, with sites spaced for privacy but no electricity.

## Food
**The Omelette Shoppe** has two locations—the corner of Cass and State, (616) 946-0912, and Front Street in Campus Plaza, (616) 946-0590—offering a breakfast, brunch, and lunch menu with emphasis on inexpensive, healthful foods. Everything is prepared without preservatives or additives: 29 omelet selections, whole grain cereals, French toast, fresh fruits, pancakes, muffins, rolls, and breads baked daily. Their coffee is excellent. Two East Front Street eateries, **Soho Cafe**, 439 East Front Street, and **Stone Soup**, 115 East Front Street, (616) 941-1190, serve inexpensive and tasty soups, salads, and sandwiches for lunch Monday through Saturday. **Reflections**, atop the Waterfront Inn, 2061 U.S. 31 North, (616) 938-2321, serves savory American fare, specializing in fresh fish and seafood. Reflections features an outstanding view of East Bay and Old Mission Peninsula. Open seven days a week for lunch and dinner, with brunch on Sunday, and entertainment Friday and Saturday nights.

For exceptional dining, try the **Bowers Harbor Inn**, 13512 Peninsula Drive, Old Mission Peninsula, (616) 223-4222. Built in 1880 as a family mansion by a Chicago industrialist, the inn has won national recognition since 1974 for its excellent cuisine and extensive wine list.

In Leland, **The Bluebird Restaurant and Bar**, 102 East River Street, (616) 256-9081, east of the M-22 bridge, is open Easter through October, serving moderately priced lunch and dinner daily. Fresh whitefish is the specialty, and there is a good selection of local, California, and European wines.

**The Cove**, 111 River Street, in Fishtown, (616) 256-9834, has dinner entrées priced between $7 and $15, and it specializes in fresh local whitefish and perch. The Cove has a large outdoor deck overlooking Lake Michigan. Open for lunch and dinner daily, May 15 through October.

# SLEEPING BEAR DUNES NATIONAL LAKESHORE TO GRAYLING

Drive and hike up towering dunes in Sleeping Bear Dunes National Lakeshore for views of glacier-sculpted landscape and offshore islands. Drive east to Grayling to explore central Michigan's forests and lakes. Canoe and fish for trout in the one of the great rivers of North America or in one of the region's most beautiful, bluest, and cleanest lakes. Commune with nature in one of the last magnificent stands of virgin white pine in Michigan. For campers, North Higgins Lake State Park is an ideal rest and recreation spot.

## Suggested Schedule

| | |
|---|---|
| 7:00 a.m. | Early breakfast. |
| 8:00 a.m. | Stop at Empire Visitor Interpretive Center. |
| 8:30 a.m. | Drive up Pierce Stocking Scenic Drive. |
| 10:30 a.m. | Climb Sleeping Bear Dune. |
| 11:30 a.m. | Drive to the Interlochen Center for the Arts for a picnic lunch and tour. |
| 2:00 p.m. | Take M-72 to Grayling. |
| 4:00 p.m. | Visit the Logging Museum in Hartwick Pines State Park and walk on Virgin Pines Forest Foot Trail. |
| 5:30 p.m. | Visit North Higgins Lake State Park. |
| 7:30 p.m. | Relaxation, dinner, and early to bed. |

**Travel Route: Leland to North Higgins Lake State Park (160 miles)**

Follow Highway 22 to Glen Arbor and continue on Highway 22 across Glen Lake to the Empire Visitor Center, then head north on Highway 22 and left on M-109 just a few miles to the entrance to Pierce Stocking Scenic Drive. Return to M-109, turn left, and drive about 2 miles to the parking area for the Sleeping Bear Dune Climb. Afterward, turn back toward Empire and take Highway 22

south. Turn left on Indian Hill Road to Honor and take 31
east to the Interlochen turnoff. At this point you're 38
miles from Empire and you have driven about 75 miles.

Continue on Highway 31/37 17 miles to Traverse City.
From Traverse City it's another 55 to 60 miles on M-72 to
Grayling, Hartwick Pines State Park, and North Higgins
Lake State Park. To go directly to North Higgins Lake State
Park, from M-72 get on I-75, which divides shortly; take
U.S. 27 toward Lansing. Five miles south get off at CR 203
(Old M-76) and turn east (left) to North Higgins Lake State
Park. The entrance to the park is about a half mile from
the intersection with Old 27.

**Sleeping Bear Dunes National Lakeshore**
A Chippewa Indian legend tells the story of a bear and her
two cubs who were driven into Lake Michigan by a raging
forest fire. They swam and swam, but the cubs tired and
lagged behind. The mother bear climbed a bluff to watch
and wait for the cubs, but the cubs drowned. Sleeping
Bear Dune is a solitary dune that marks the spot where
the mother bear waited. The Manitou Islands offshore are
the cubs.

Located on the northwestern shore of Michigan's Lower
Peninsula, Sleeping Bear Dunes National Lakeshore comprises a hilly region fringed with massive coastal sand
dunes and dotted with clear lakes. The 40 miles of the
park between Platte Bay and Good Harbor Bay is a
diverse landscape—birch-lined streams, dense beech
and maple forests, and rugged sand dune bluffs towering
on headlands as high as 480 feet.

Pick up a self-guiding brochure, detailed maps, and lots
of other information at the Empire Visitor Interpretive
Center, P.O. Box 277, Empire, MI 49630, (616) 326-5134.
The visitor center is open daily all year.

**Sightseeing Highlights**
**▲▲▲ Pierce Stocking Scenic Drive**—About three
miles north of the center, the scenic drive leaves M-109
for a 7½-mile loop around to the top of forested dunes.

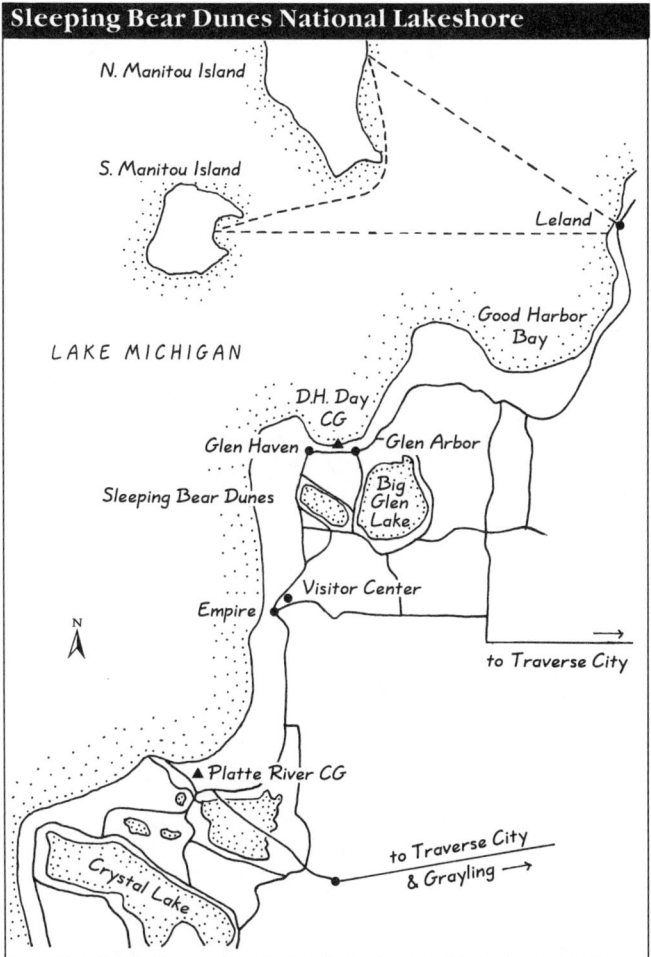

**Sleeping Bear Dunes National Lakeshore**

N. Manitou Island

S. Manitou Island

Leland

LAKE MICHIGAN

Good Harbor Bay

D.H. Day CG

Glen Haven

Glen Arbor

Big Glen Lake

Sleeping Bear Dunes

Visitor Center

Empire

N

→ to Traverse City

▲ Platte River CG

to Traverse City & Grayling →

Crystal Lake

The drive is open mid-May to early November, weather permitting. Bicycles are permitted. Observation platforms and picnic areas dot the crest.

▲ **Sleeping Bear Dune Climb**—A few miles north of the scenic drive, you can climb Sleeping Bear. The dune climb is a strenuous but rewarding feat. There are two trails at the top: a dunes trail (4 miles) and a loop trail (nearly 3 miles). There is no water or shelter from the sun and wind. Children should be supervised. Although it may look tempting to walk barefoot in the sand, hikers should wear shoes to protect their feet.

▲▲ **Interlochen Center for the Arts**—This world-famous facility offers instruction in all aspects of music, visual arts, theater and dance, and regularly scheduled performances each summer by students and internationally known professional artists. Concerts in the summer of 1990 featured Jean-Pierre Rampal, the world's pre-eminent flutist; New Orleans' Pete Fountain and his jazz band; the Oak Ridge Boys; the Paul Winter Consort; Bluegrass Festival; Itzak Perlman, the great violinist; John Denver; and many more. The center is near **Interlochen State Park** (see below). From U.S. 31, go south on M-137. Concerts are scheduled from late June to mid-August and late September to May. (616) 276-9221. At Interlochen State Park, you'll find hundreds of campers who set up tents, RVs, and trailers to attend Interlochen events just one mile north of the park.

**Grayling and the Au Sable River**

Grayling primarily services a National Guard camp, hunters, annual droves of morel mushroom pickers and trout fishermen, and others enjoying the great woods and lakes of central Michigan. In particular, visitors come for the beautiful **Au Sable River**, which flows through the 415,000-acre **Huron National Forest**. Fishing for brook trout, rainbows, and brown trout on this legendary river has to be one of the greatest fishing experiences in North America. The so-called "Holy Waters" of the Au Sable begin at **Burton's Landing**, about 2½ miles on M-72 or about 10 miles by canoe on the Au Sable River from **Penrod's** canoe rentals in Grayling, (517) 348-2910. **Borchers**, (517) 345-4921, on Maple Street, and **Carlyle Canoes**, (517) 348-2301, on State Street, are within a mile of each other along the river.

▲▲ **Hartwick Pines State Park**—In the forests of Hartwick, (517) 348-7068, 7½ miles northeast of Grayling on M-93, you can see what northern Michigan looked like a century ago. The Logging Museum exhibits the story of Michigan's "gold"—more than 160 billion board feet of lumber cut from the white pine forests. Hikers in this 10,000-acre park usually can find tent camping sites.

▲▲ **Virgin Pines Forest Foot Trail**—This mile-long trail in Hartwick Pines State Park which takes you through some of the last remaining stands of white pine in the Great Lakes is a precious experience.

▲▲ **North Higgins Lake State Park**—A beautiful beach and campground run along one of the prettiest and cleanest lakes in Michigan, with miles of hiking trails. Michigan's first forest nursery, which contributed to the replanting of hundreds of millions of trees, is in the park near the interpretive center. Trails leading to hundreds of backcountry acres begin here also.

### Lodging

Carl and Judy Craft's **North Country Lodge**, (517) 348-8471, just north of M-72W on the right side of Business Loop I-75 in Grayling, is a wonderful place to stay any season. Their pleasant knotty pine rooms and honeymoon or anniversary celebration suites are as nice as you'll find in the woods of the Great Lakes. Rates are $43 to $46 for two people in standard rooms. **Warbler's Way Inn**, (517) 348-4541, at the corner of McClellan and Maple in Grayling, is a perfectly adequate motel for $42 per night double.

### Camping

Most of the 218 campsites in **North Higgins Lake State Park**, 11511 W. Higgins Lake, Roscommon, MI 48653, (517) 821-6125, are roomy, shaded, and somewhat private. The east wing's sites (1-112) are larger and more secluded.

On the south side of the lake, **South Higgins Lake State Park**, Route 2, Box 360, Roscommon, MI 48653,

(517) 821-6374, has more beachfront than North Higgins
Lake (2 miles versus 1,500 feet) and is more crowded.
This park has tree-shaded picnic tables, a bathhouse and
camp store, and 512 modern, tree-shaded sites, with very
little privacy. Lots 203-512 are newer. There's one mile
of campers-only beach. Reservations months in advance
are practical, especially for weekends. Only half the sites
are reserved. Without reservations, you have to get there
very early and wait for openings. There are good hiking
areas across CR 104 (Marl Lake). The park store has rental
rowboats, canoes, and pedalboats. Bring fishing gear for
the perch, lake and brown trout, and smallmouth bass.

The modern lots (1-42) with electrical hookups in
**Hartwick Pines State Park**, Route 3, Box 3840, Grayling, MI 49738, (517) 348-7068, are well-shaded and as
good as any in the Higgins Lakes parks. At Hartwick, you
are surrounded by thousands of acres of scenic woodlands. Reach the entrance from M-93 west from Grayling.

**Food**

In Glenn Arbor, **Julie's Restaurant**, (517) 334-3428, is
an inexpensive family restaurant open daily for breakfast,
lunch, and dinner from Memorial Day to Labor Day. For
casual dining with an excellent view of the lake, there's
**The Landing at Glen Arbor** on Lake Street, (517)
334-4640.

In Grayling, try oat bran pancakes for breakfast at the
**Lone Pine**. **Bear's Country Inn** is fine for any meal.
Both are on Maple near the Warbler's Way Inn. Near
Higgins Lake, big coffee rolls are a specialty at **Big Mac's
Market**. The **Hut Restaurant** across CR 200 near Hig-
gins Lake will do nicely for convenience. I suggest that
you buy a picnic lunch at a local supermarket on
U.S. 27 and head for one of the state parks. The **Cut
River Restaurant**, (517) 821-9521, east of South Higgins
Lake State Park, serves beef, fish, chicken, veal, pork,
tacos, pizza, and other basic dishes for a very reasonable
price. From the restaurant, it's about five miles on CR 100
to get to I-75 south.

# FRANKENMUTH TO FLINT AND PORT HURON

Bavarian food and atmosphere around Frankenmuth provide the main attraction in a day of driving to Port Huron, your stopover en route to Detroit or possibly Ontario, Canada, and Niagara Falls.

## Suggested Schedule

| | |
|---|---|
| 9:30 a.m. | Check out of Grayling and head for Frankenmuth. |
| 11:30 a.m. | Frankenmuth touring. |
| 12:30 p.m. | Lunch in Frankenmuth. |
| 2:00 p.m. | Leave Frankenmuth. |
| 3:00 p.m. | Visit Flint's Sloan Museum and the Flint Institute of Arts. |
| 5:00 p.m. | Leave for Port Huron. |
| 6:00 p.m. | Arrive in Port Huron and check in at the Victorian Inn. |
| 7:15 p.m. | Dinner at the Victorian Inn. |

**Travel Route: Grayling to Port Huron (210 miles)**
From Grayling, drive south around Higgins Lake, just for the scenery, and take I-75 south at the Houghton Lake entrance. After passing the Standish exit, don't get off I-75 with the idea of driving along Saginaw Bay, because you can't. The closest you can get to Saginaw Bay is around Bay City.

From I-75, take Exit 144 and drive five miles east (left) to Frankenmuth. Leaving Frankenmuth, take M-83 south for five miles and turn right on M-54/M-83 past Mount Morris (and signs for Huckleberry Railroad & Crossroads Village at Bray Road). Get on I-75 at Exit 136, drive south to Exit 8A on I-475, Longway Boulevard, pass under I-475, and take a left on Forest Street to the Sloan Museum. Park on your right. From Flint, get on I-69E to Port Huron, then M-25, turn left on Court, and left again on 7th to Union to get to the Victorian Inn.

## Frankenmuth

Founded by German settlers about 150 years ago,
Frankenmuth has remained a "Little Bavaria" ever
since—with Old World architecture of half-timbered
chalets, gingerbread decorations, gift shops, flower
decorations, and other attractions. Listen to the 36-bell
**Bavarian Inn Glockenspiel Tower** at 11:00 a.m., noon,
3:00 p.m., 6:00 p.m., 9:00 p.m., and 10:00 p.m., and
watch the accompanying figurine movement. Photo-
graph **Zehnder's Holz-Brucke** (covered bridge) across
the Cass River, and enjoy a family-style, all-you-can-eat
chicken dinner at the enormous Bavarian Inn or Zehnder's Restaurant.

   **The Frankenmuth Bavarian Festival** takes place at
Heritage Park during the second week of June. The hours
are noon to midnight, except for Sunday, when the hours
are 2:00 p.m. to midnight. There is dancing, bands, other
live entertainment, and heaps of bratwurst, pretzels,
sauerkraut, chicken dinners, beer, and more.

### Sightseeing Highlights

▲ **Bronner's Christmas Wonderland**—One of the
biggest attractions in Michigan, Bronner's recently doubled in size to guarantee its position as the world's largest
ornament retailer. Christmas in July is alive and well at
Bronner's. From June 1 to December 24, hours are 9:00 a.m.
to 9:00 p.m. weekdays, 9:00 a.m. to 1:00 p.m. Saturdays,
and noon to 7:00 p.m. Sundays. The rest of the year,
hours are 9:00 a.m. to 5:30 p.m. Monday through Thursday and Saturday, 9:00 a.m. to 9:00 p.m. Friday, and
1:00 to 5:30 p.m. Sunday. Bronner's is on Highway 83,
one mile south of the Heileman Brewery.

▲ **Frankenmuth Historical Museum**—Featuring local
history from 1840, when German settlers tried spreading
Christianity among the Chippewa, the museum is near
the Chamber of Commerce and the Fischer Opera House
on S. Main.

## "The Thumb"

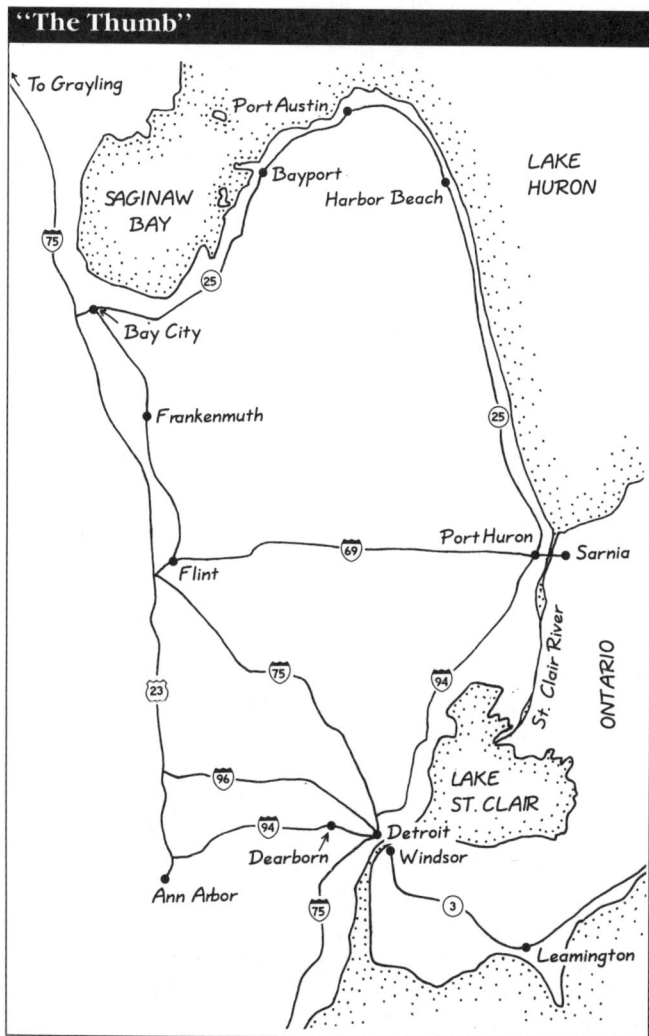

## Flint

Once the giant in GM's automobile manufacturing kingdom, making all of the Buicks and Chevrolets in America,

Flint today is a depressed city with a few exceptional attractions.

▲▲ **Alfred P. Sloan Museum**—This museum contains displays of Flint's history as a lumbering town, its early auto years, and its transformation into an auto capital. There's a display of vintage automobiles that everyone can enjoy, and special exhibits from time to time. The fourth week in June, a 1,000-vehicle antique auto show is held at the museum. Address and hours: 1221 E. Kearsley in Flint's Cultural Center, (313) 762-1169; Tuesday through Friday 10:00 a.m. to 5:00 p.m., Saturday and Sunday noon to 5:00 p.m., and on Monday in July and August. Admission is $3.50 for adults and $3 for children and students.

▲ **Flint Institute of Arts**—This facility displays an outstanding collection of nineteenth-century French paintings (Corot, Courbet, Renoir, Toulouse-Lautrec, and others) and a wide variety of temporary exhibits sponsored by generous local patrons. Address and hours: 1120 Kearsley, (313) 234-1695; Tuesday through Saturday 10:00 a.m. to 5:00 p.m., Sunday 1:00 to 5:00 p.m.

▲ **GM Truck and Bus Flint Assembly Plant Tour**— The tour of this 3-million-square-foot assembly plant is leisurely. The pieces of the chassis are assembled mostly by workers, rather than robots as in the Buick City Tour. The body is swung down onto the chassis the way it has been done for decades, with a team of workers securing the two sections. You can expect to see about 5,000 workers making some Blazers and pickup trucks Tuesdays and Thursdays only, 9:30 and 11:30 a.m., (313) 236-4978. Take I-75 south to the Bristol Road exit, turn left (east) to Van Slyke, and turn into the plant.

▲ **Buick City Tour**—An amazing contrast to the GM Truck and Bus Flint Assembly Plant Tour, the Buick City tour shows you a fully integrated auto assembly plant in a 450-acre, two-mile-long facility. Sophisticated robots perform the toughest jobs at a brisk pace in conjunction with a computer-guided assembly line. Tours are about 1½ hours long, on Tuesdays and Thursdays at 9:30 a.m.

and noon. Take I-475 north and exit at Hamilton to 902 E. Hamilton. (313) 238-4484.

## Port Huron

First there was Fort Joseph, then Fort Gratiot, then Port Huron, one of the oldest towns in the state. Nearby **Fort Gratiot Lighthouse** (1825) is the oldest navigational light in the state. Port Huron is best known as the connecting point to Canada by rail. Young Tom Edison sold snacks and papers on the Port Huron-Detroit train to finance his laboratory in the train's baggage car, until he was fired for accidentally setting fire to it.

## Lodging

If you decide to stay over in Frankenmuth for the **Frankenmuth Bavarian Festival**, several pleasant and inexpensive ($35 to $45 single and double) B&Bs are located near the center of town: Kathy and Louie Weiss's **Bavarian Town B&B**, (517) 652-8057; Richard and Donna Hodge's **Bed and Breakfast at the Pines**, (517) 652-9019; and Margaret Kueffner's **Kueffner Haus B&B**, (517) 652-6839.

Port Huron's **Victorian Inn**, 1229 7th at Union, 2 blocks west of M-25, (313) 984-1437, is a beautifully refurbished Queen Anne house, in the pretty Bluewater area. Lynne Secory operates the Victorian as a four-room B&B and respected restaurant for lunches and dinners. (See Food, below.) Rates are $50 for double rooms with shared bath or $60 for a private bath; continental breakfast is included. Relax in the cellar pub before dinner. Union is one way from M-25, so turn west on Court and take 7th south to Union.

## Camping

**Lakeport State Park**, Route 1, Port Huron, MI 48060, (313) 327-6765, stretches 1½ miles along the scenic Lake Huron shoreline, three miles north of Port Huron. The campground is north of Lakeport. Of the 365 sites, lots 1 to 300 are farthest from the highway and closest to the

beach. These are small sites, shaded but lacking privacy.
Try to get lots 16 to 46 for the best views. Sites 301-365
are larger, with paved slips but even less privacy. The
whole campground is heavily used from June to Labor
Day, so make reservations early.

**Food**
In Frankenmuth, **Zehnders** is fine for a light lunch and
the pastry is hard to beat if you can cope with the crowds.
Sausage fans should stop at **Kern's, Willi's Sausages**, or
**Bernthal Packing**.

In Flint, stop at the **Windmill Place**, 877 E. Fifth at
Saginaw, just north of downtown Flint, a two-level court
with 13 good eateries.

The **Victorian Inn** in Port Huron is known for its
American cuisine as well as its ambience and service.
Lunch and dinner are served in a 50-seat restaurant in this
Queen Ann House at 1229 7th at Union, (313) 984-1437.
Dinner is served from 5:30 to 8:30 p.m.

**Itinerary Option**
Instead of driving to Frankenmuth and Flint, drive
around the Thumb to **Port Austin** and nearby **Port
Crescent State Park**, with 47 campsites on white sandy
beaches along the water (1775 Port Austin Road, Port
Austin, MI 48467, 517-738-8663). Check out the
**Questover Inn** or the **Garfield Inn**, a National Historic
Site, in Port Austin. Both B&Bs are owned by Gail Regnier
and feature double rooms for $50, (517) 738-5253.

Continuing around the Thumb to Port Huron, you'll
pass historic **Port Sanilac** with more than 40 buildings
over 100 years old, and **Lakeport State Park** three miles
north of Port Huron, where the lake flows into the St.
Clair River. (See Camping, above.)

## PORT HURON—NIAGARA FALLS (ONTARIO AND NEW YORK)— DETROIT

From Port Huron, you are less than 200 miles and about four hours of easy driving from spectacular Niagara Falls and the scenic Niagara Parkway between Lakes Erie and Ontario. If you have at least three days to spare, the drive through southwestern Ontario along the shorelines of these lakes, past a string of picturesque little coastal towns and park reserves, reveals a completely different glimpse of the Great Lakes. See Niagara Falls from both sides of the border with Canada—close up from above, below, and in the middle, day and night—and you'll understand why it merits being one of the most popular tourist destinations in the world.

**Entering Canada:** Passports to enter Canada or return to the United States are not required of U.S. citizens. Carry proof of citizenship (birth certificate or voter's cer- tification) and proof of residence (such as a valid U.S. driver's license). If you're driving a rented car, be sure to have the contract. If the car is not yours, carry written proof from the owners showing that you have permission to drive their car. Short-term trip accident coverage is recommended. Ask your insurance agent about a Canadian Non-Resident Inter-Provincial Motor Vehicle Liability Insurance Card.

Remember that you can claim a refund on sales tax paid on goods and services in Ontario, including accom- modations (but not meals except AP or MAP), if the amount claimed is more than $7. When you enter Ontario, request a brochure covering procedures for obtaining provincial sales tax refunds. All prices indicated below are in Canadian dollars.

**Getting There:** This extension leaves the main route in Port Huron, crosses the Canadian border into Sarnia and heads out Highway 402 around the south side of London to the turnoff to Highway 4 south to St. Thomas and Port Stanley. After lunch and a stroll in Port Stanley, take coastal Route 24 to the village of Port Bruce, and then Route 73 to Highway 3. (If you have the time, stay on Route 24 along the Lake Erie coast through Port Burwell, Long Point, and other pleasant villages and scenery.) Drive east again on Highway 3 from Aylmer to Fort Erie in order to get on the Niagara Parkway into Niagara.

From Sarnia to London, it's 64 miles and 1 hour 10 minutes, and from London to Niagara, it's 125 miles (direct) and 2 hours 30 minutes, for a total of 189 miles and 3 hours and 40 minutes of uninterrupted driving. Following the suggested scenic route from Port Stanley eastward along the Lake Erie shoreline adds at least one hour of driving plus whatever time you spend sightseeing.

From Niagara, your destination is St. Catharines and the Welland Canal. From St. Catharines, get on the QEW and drive past Hamilton to the spectacular Royal Botanical Gardens. Afterward, your destinations are Leamington, Windsor, and Detroit. Turn southwest on Highway 403 to Woodstock, where you take Highway 401 to Highway 4, south of London, connecting to Highway 3, which follows the coast to Blenheim and Leamington, then turn northwest to Windsor. From Leamington, it's less than an hour to Detroit on Highway 3, with a choice of entering Detroit over the Ambassador Bridge or through the Detroit-Windsor Tunnel, which gets you closer to the heart of downtown Detroit's riverfront attractions.

In Detroit, you pick up the main route again by driving to the Detroit Institute of the Arts on I-375, to I-75 north to the Warren exit, west on Warren to Woodward, and turning left toward Wayne State University and the Cultural Center complex, or exit I-94 at John R/Woodward exit and proceed south on John R four blocks to Farnsworth. An alternative is to get on I-75 east to I-10 north to the Wayne State University exit at Forest, turn right to Woodward, then left on Woodward to the Detroit Institute of Arts. Park at the DIA's underground garage on Farnsworth.

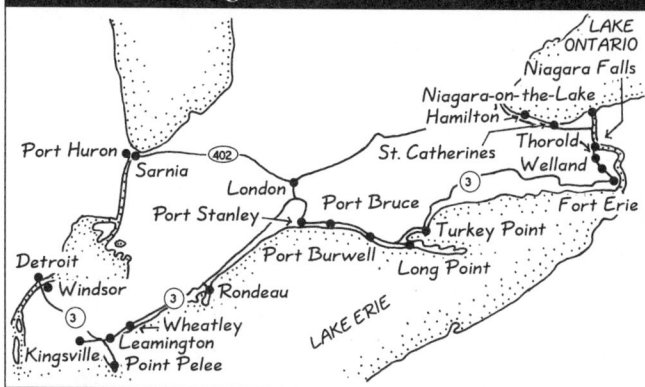

**Port Huron—Niagara Falls—Detroit**

### First Day: Port Huron to Port Stanley (84 miles)

Before leaving Port Huron and crossing the **Blue Water Bridge** to Sarnia, Ontario, see some of the city's historic sites clustered around the bridge, such as the **1858 Grand Trunk Depot**, off Thomas Edison Parkway, fronting on the St. Clair River, where young Tom Edison started tinkering. View Lake Huron from **Lighthouse Park**, five blocks north of the bridge. **Port Huron Museum of Arts and History**, 1115 Sixth Street between Wall and Court, one block west of M-25, Wednesday to Sunday 1:00 to 4:30 p.m., has a really interesting collection of Indian artifacts and marine paraphernalia rescued from the lake by divers and models of Forts Joseph and Gratiot, lots of natural history, furniture, and other things of interest.

   **Sarnia** can boast of Canada's largest collection of roses (Rosebud Gardens) and scenic **St. Clair Parkway** along the St. Clair River. Unfortunately, depending on the wind, the air in the city can be unpleasantly polluted with petrochemical odors.

   If you have an extra day and evening, I recommend seeing one of Canada's best collections of regional historical exhibits in a variety of locations inside and outside of

**London** on the way to Port Stanley or on the way back
from Niagara Falls. The **Ska-Nah-Doht Indian Village**
contains 16 structures re-creating a prehistoric Iroquoian
village, located in the Longwoods Road Conservation
Area on Highway 2 near where the road intersects with
Highway 402 at Delaware. The **Royal Canadian Regi-
ment Museum** is housed in Wolseley Hall, Wolseley
Barracks, Oxford and Elizabeth streets. Get on Richmond
Street north to Oxford Street and turn right (east) for
about 10 blocks. Keep going east on Oxford to Clarke
Side Road, take a left to Fanshawe Park Road and a right to
the **Fanshawe Park and Pioneer Village**, a re-creation
of an Ontario farm village with craft demonstrations.
Return to town and, in the afternoon, see the **London
Regional Art and Historical Museums** along the
Thames River, 421 Rideout Street North, 9:00 a.m. to
5:00 p.m. Tuesday through Sunday, between Queens
Avenue and Dundas Street. In the evening, just a few
blocks away, attend a performance at the beautifully
restored **Grand Theatre**, 471 Richmond Street, (519)
672-8800. The alternative is the overnight recommenda-
tion in Port Stanley.

From Port Huron or London, head for Port Stanley, 28
miles south of London. Once a famous tourists' playground, Port Stanley is being rediscovered and refurbished. The local specialty shops, art galleries, and
several artists' studios up and down Main Street make
browsing really fun. On Bridge Street, taste buds beware
of delicious homemade items in Shaw's Bakery, Broder-
ick's Ice Cream Parlor, and Stanley's Chocolates and
Things. Located in the Town Hall, the **Port Stanley
Summer Theatre**, (519) 782-3315, puts on three plays
each summer, starting the last week in June.

I encourage you to spend a night in Port Stanley (see
Where to Stay, below, for an exceptional overnight
choice). Take a self-guided **Historical Walking Tour**
(call Jim Sorrenti for a brochure at 519-782-3550). Cross
over the Lift Bridge to the **Port Stanley Terminal Rail**
and take a 45-minute train ride to the Village of Union

and back. The train runs Tuesday to Saturday hourly in the afternoon from 1:00 to 3:00 p.m., Sunday until 4:00 p.m. Fares: adults $5, children 12 and under $2.50. Across from the station, take a one-hour cruise on Kettle Creek and Lake Erie aboard the **Kettle Creek Queen**, (519) 782-3315, at 1:30 p.m. and 3:30 p.m. every day except Monday.

Drive the country roads leading out of town, like scenic Route 20 to Fingal and Shedden (or save this drive for the return trip when you are heading for Highway 3 to Windsor). Walk the **Elgin Hiking Trail**, which follows Kettle Creek to St. Thomas, or climb **Invererie Heights** for a spectacular view of Lake Erie. For bird-watchers, **Hawk Cliff** is a must, as it is one of the largest flyways on the continent for migrating raptors.

Josie of **Josie's Braided Mats**, 350 Warren Street, (519) 782-3458, makes some of the finest braided mats you'll find in the Great Lakes. **Floridel Gardens**, 330 George Street, (519) 782-4015, with over 10,000 orchid plants to choose from, is a match for any wholesale florist. At the corner of William and Smith streets in a mid-nineteenth-century home is **Kid's Port of Call**, one of the most creative children's toys and clothing stores you will see anywhere. On the north edge of town on Highway 4, **Moore Water Gardens** is the largest supplier of aquatic plants and water lilies in Canada and welcomes visitors daily 9:00 a.m. to 5:00 p.m.

**Lodging:** With the help of a very talented local architect, Hal Sorrenti, innkeepers Gary and Jean Vedova have transformed **The Kettle Creek Inn**, Main Street, Port Stanley, Ontario N0L 2A0, (519) 782-3388, into one of the most attractive B&Bs in the Great Lakes. The original 1849 inn has 10 guest rooms, first-class central washrooms, and a sauna. The addition of two new buildings (containing eight comfortably furnished suites, three with a whirlpool) around a landscaped courtyard and the original blue clapboard building, a tastefully decorated dining room, pub, cozy library, and parlor with wood burning fireplace, creates an intimate sanctuary. All of the rooms in the inn display paintings by Elgin County artists. Room rates range from $60 to $135 double occupancy.

**Port Burwell Provincial Park** has the nearest camping with 232 sites in over 550 pleasant, tree-shaded lakeshore acres for $10.25 per family. (The park closes by mid-October.) You'll find a small grocery and a coin-operated laundry. For fewer sites (90) in a much larger park, continue to the over 1,000-acre **Backus Conservation Area**, (519) 428-4623, in Port Rowan (on Regional Rd. 42) for $9 per family but only 30 sites with electrical and water hookups ($2). All of these camping facilities are located along scenic coastal roads.

**Food:** Have lunch at any of Port Stanley's restaurants, all within walking distance of each other: the **Harborside** at Clifton, 210 Main Street; **Jackson's Wharf**, 208 Main Street; **Kelley's Boardwalk**, 128 William Street; **Schneider's Pizza Restaurant**, 170 William Street; and the **Lakeview Restaurant**, 301 Bridge. Save the **Kettle Creek Inn** for dinner. The Inn's restaurant serves delicious food, and the service is friendly and attentive. In good weather there's dining on the patio or in the courtyard's gazebo.

### Second Day: To and in Niagara Falls (145 miles)

**Getting There:** From Port Stanley, drive on Route 24 to Route 36 to **Sparta**, Canada's oldest Quaker settlement, with 22 historic buildings, a wonderful tearoom, and a chance to meet Peter Robson, Canada's foremost watercolorist, and perhaps watch him work at his gallery and home, **Studio Sparta**, Main Street, (519) 775-2522. Then drive up Route 42 to Point Dover and take Highway 6 to Highway 3 east toward Welland. East of Port Bruce, 50-foot cliffs extend along churning Lake Erie as far as the eye can see. Nine miles east of Port Burwell, sand hills tower 450 feet above the lake. Pass through the fishing and duck hunting resort of Port Rowen and the **Backus Conservation Area and Historical Complex**, with a

1798 mill still producing flour. Twenty-mile-long **Long Point Provincial Park** has an excellent beach and bird-watching areas. Drive by the very pretty Turkey Point resort area and 782-acre **Turkey Point Provincial Park** (in which you can camp). Picturesque Port Dover, one of the largest freshwater fishing ports in the world, has hundreds of colorful fishing vessels in its harbor and a **Harbor Museum** with hundreds of artifacts depicting the fishing industry on Lake Erie. **Rock Point Provincial Park** has another good beach. From Port Colborne drive 12 miles to **Fort Erie** where you get on scenic **Niagara Parkway** to Niagara Falls. In Fort Erie, visit **Old Fort Erie** where Lake Erie empties into the Niagara River on its way to Lake Ontario. The fort has an extensive collection of antique artifacts.

**Getting Around Niagara:** Traffic in Niagara Falls can get very congested, especially in the main tourist areas during the summer. My suggested plan is to stay in Niagara Falls on the Canadian side, check into your accommodations near the falls, and walk or take buses to the main observation points during the day, at night, and the next morning. Have dinner in Niagara at an observation point near your accommodations. Shift to the New York side for a few hours, mainly to see Goat Island and views of the falls from there. Back on scenic Niagara Parkway in Ontario after that, you concentrate on seeing the power, beauty, and majesty of the falls and river from different vantage points between Rainbow Bridge and Lake Ontario.

The Niagara Parks Commission People Mover System makes it easy and inexpensive to move around by bus. It operates from mid-May to mid-October, providing service every few minutes between Rapids View Parking Area and just past the Rainbow Bridge and back, for an all-day fare of only $1.50 for adults and $.75 for children.

**What to See:** The cities of Niagara Falls, Ontario, and Niagara Falls, New York, are connected by the **Rainbow Bridge** near the middle of one of the shortest and wildest rivers in the world. Niagara's rapids reach a speed of

30 miles per hour. The Canadian falls are 160 feet high, and the crest extends over 2,000 feet in a deep curve, earning them the name of Horseshoe Falls. The American falls are slightly higher but less than 1,000 feet wide, straight, and somewhat less spectacular. Bridal Veil, the smallest of the three cataracts, is separated from the American falls by **Luna Island**. **Goat Island** divides the American and Canadian falls.

**Queen Victoria Park** has great views of the falls and beautiful floral displays. **The Table Rock House** at the park contains an elevator that descends for a close-up view of the Canadian Horseshoe Falls and the Niagara River. The observation plaza is about 25 feet above the river. Open until 11:00 p.m. from mid-June to Labor Day. Adults, $3.85; children 6 to 12, $1.90. In this park you'll also find the **Horseshoe Incline Railway** leading to the **Maid of the Mists** boat dock. The park is lighted in the evening so that you can take an after-dinner stroll.

Maid of the Mists boats enter Horseshoe Basin and pass in front of the falls. Take the incline railway down to the dock for 75 cents. Catch the boat at the foot of Clifton Hill Street. Starting at 9:00 a.m., the boats run every 15 minutes from June 27 to Labor Day and every half hour from mid-May to June 27 and Labor Day to October 31. Adult fare, $6.50; children 6 to 12, $3.65.

**The Whirlpool Rapids** of the Niagara River are an incredible spectacle. Take the **Great Gorge Adventure**, north of the Whirlpool Rapids Bridge along the Parkway. An elevator takes you down to a boardwalk where you can stroll along the rapids. In July and August, you can go down until 8:00 p.m.; after Labor Day, until 7:30 p.m. Adults, $3.70; children 6-12, $1.85.

The **Spanish Aero Car** (or Whirlpool Aerocar) is a cable car carrying passengers high over Niagara Gorge and churning Whirlpool Basin and back on a 1,600-foot-long cableway. Open daily 9:00 a.m. to dusk; adults $3.35, children ages 6-12 $1.65. The car leaves near the intersection of Victoria Avenue and Niagara Parkway, north of the Whirlpool Bridge.

## Niagara Falls, Canada

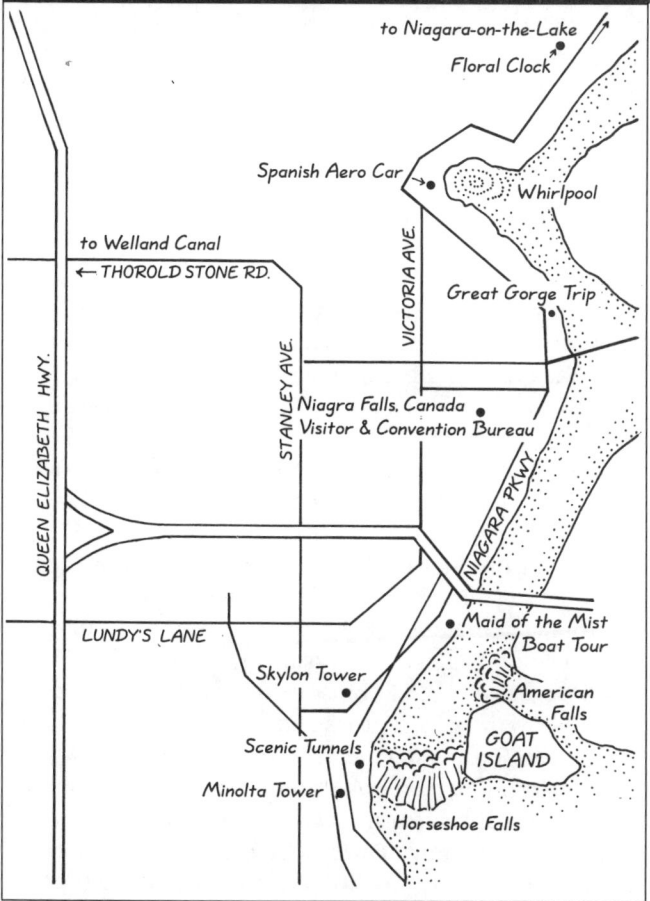

*to Niagara-on-the-Lake*

*Floral Clock*

*Spanish Aero Car*

*Whirlpool*

*to Welland Canal*

*← THOROLD STONE RD.*

*VICTORIA AVE.*

*Great Gorge Trip*

*STANLEY AVE.*

*Niagra Falls, Canada*
*Visitor & Convention Bureau*

*QUEEN ELIZABETH HWY.*

*NIAGARA PKWY.*

*LUNDY'S LANE*

*Maid of the Mist*
*Boat Tour*

*Skylon Tower*

*American*
*Falls*

*Scenic Tunnels*

*GOAT*
*ISLAND*

*Minolta Tower*

*Horseshoe Falls*

Goat Island, surrounded by the Niagara River, can be
reached from the Rainbow Bridge via Prospect Street. En
route to Goat Island from the Rainbow Bridge, off Rainbow Boulevard, the **Turtle Native American Center
for the Living Arts** contains a museum and art gallery
of Native American heritage. Open daily 9:00 a.m. to
6:00 p.m., May through September. Walk to the island on
a pedestrian bridge from the end of Prospect Street or

drive there on Rainbow Boulevard. Drives and walks on
the island offer spectacular views of both falls. **The
Three Sisters Islands** and **Luna Island** are accessible
from Goat Island by footbridges.

At some point, perhaps for dinner, head up **Minolta
Tower-Centre**, which rises over 600 feet above the base
of the falls and 300 feet above ground level. Three dining
rooms, three open decks, and an enclosed observation
deck overlook the falls. From Victoria Park, it's only a
short distance to the tower.

Theater buffs will want to spend a relaxing evening in
picturesque, historic **Niagara-by-the-Lake** and attend
the world's only theater devoted exclusively to plays written in the era of George Bernard Shaw.

**Lodging:** Opposite the Minolta Tower, **Horseshoe
Falls Motor Inn**, 5481 Dunn Street, (416) 358-9353, has
the best price for a centrally located motel at $68.50 to
$99.50. The Travelodge's **Colonial Inn by the Falls**,
5591 Victoria Ave., (416) 367-1626 and (800) 263-2552, is
one block from Victoria Park and couldn't be more central for all of your evening and morning activities. The
six-story atrium hotel also has an indoor pool, jacuzzi,
and whirlpool. Rates in season are $89 to $119. Stay at the
**Old Stone Inn**, 5425 Robinson Street, (800) 263-8967,
also close to the falls, and ask about a Shaw Festival theater package. Room rates are $95.50 to $119.50 double.

**Camping:** Between 3 and 12 miles west of Niagara
Falls along Highway 20 are several good tent and trailer
park choices. **Niagara Falls KOA Kampground**, 8625
Lundy's Lane, (416) 356-2267, is the closest. It is a big (24
acres, 225 tent/RV and 110 RV sites), mostly open, grassy
facility with some heavily wooded tent sites, and heated
outdoor and indoor pools, for $18 for 2 persons, $5 each
extra person, $3.50 for electricity and water hookups.
Nearby **Campark Resorts**, 9387 Lundy's Lane, (416)
358-3873, is similar in size and facilities, including a
heated pool, but with fewer tent/RV sites (110, 82 with
electricity and water) and lower rates—$14 for a family of
four, with $2 for electrical and water hookups.

**Food:** The Niagara Parks Commission operates four excellent Niagara Parks restaurants, each of which has some of the best views of the falls: **Table Rock Restaurant**, right on the brink of the Canadian Falls, (416) 345-3631; **Victoria Park Restaurant**, with a patio that looks out on the American Falls, (416) 356-2217; **Queenston Heights Restaurant**, on the edge of the Niagara escarpment, 6½ miles north of the Canadian Falls, (416) 262-4274; and **Whirlpool Restaurant**, 5½ miles north of the falls. **Queenston Park** has wonderful views of the countryside from its trails, which close at dusk, and its restaurant. (Hikers will be interested to know that the park is the eastern terminus of the 450-mile **Bruce Trail**.)

The **Minolta Tower-Top of the Rainbow Dining Room**, 6732 Oakes Drive, (416) 356-1501, is a choice viewpoint to see the falls illuminated (between 9:00 p.m. and 12:30 a.m. in the summer). An alternative is the **Skylon**, 5200 Robinson Street, (416) 356-2651, with buffet-style dinners, also within walking distance of the accommodations recommended above.

**Evening Entertainment:** Niagara-on-the-Lake, where the Niagara River joins Lake Ontario, was the first capital of Upper Canada and has dozens of historic buildings dating back to the early 1800s. Only 20 minutes from Niagara Falls, some of the Great Lakes' finest wineries (Bright Wines, Inniskillin, Chateau-Gai, and Hillebrand) are located in the area. A highlight of the area is the **Shaw Festival**, specializing in plays of the George Bernard Shaw era (1856-1950) performed in three theaters within four blocks of each other. Drive along Niagara Parkway to Niagara-by-the-Lake. Along the way, see the **Niagara Parks Commission School of Horticulture**, open year-round with 100 acres of gardens; **Niagara Glen Nature Reserve**, a lovely forested spot with wooded pathways along the Niagara River and Niagara Glen Restaurant on the heights above; and the huge **Floral Clock** on River Road about a mile before the Queenston Park. Adjacent to the Floral Clock, the **Centennial Lilac**

**Garden** blooms profusely late in May with 256 varieties of lilacs.

### Third Day: Niagara Falls West to Detroit via the Welland Canal and the Royal Botanical Garden

After seeing the most famous water diversion and control project in North America, around Niagara Falls, you'll see the less well known (and fourth) Welland Canal, built to circumvent Niagara Falls and connect Lakes Erie and Ontario. The best place to see the Welland Canal is Lock #3 in St. Catharines. Afterward, visit Old Port Dalhousie that grew up around the first canal (opened in 1829). Drive to the Royal Botanical Gardens (RBG) in Hamilton to spend several hours in vast flower gardens or walks on nature trails. From the RBG, it's a few hours of driving to Leamington. Stretch your legs on the Marsh Boardwalk in Point Pelee National Park. Leamington offers some excellent dinner choices. From Leamington, it's only 26 miles to Detroit via the Detroit-Windsor Tunnel.

  **Getting There:** In Niagara, Ontario, take Victoria Avenue to Bridge Street, turn left and then right on Stanley Avenue to Thorold Stone Road. Follow Thorold Stone Road across the QEW and the Welland Canal to Pine Street. Take a right on Richmond and follow Glendale Avenue, then a left at Canal Road to Lock #3 on the canal and the Viewing Centre (elevated viewing platform) in St. Catharines.

  From St. Catharines, get on the QEW and drive past Hamilton across the Burlington Skyway Bridge. Exit the QEW at Plains Road, turn left at the traffic light, and watch for signs for the spectacular Royal Botanical Gardens. Leaving the Royal Botanical Gardens, turn southwest on Highway 403 to Woodstock, where you'll take Highway 401 to Highway 4 south of London. Highway 4 connects to Highway 3, which follows the coast to Blenheim, Leamington, and Windsor. From Leamington, it's less than an hour to Detroit on Highway 3, with a choice of entering Detroit over the Ambassador Bridge or through the Detroit-Windsor Tunnel.

The Detroit-Windsor Tunnel is a much less pleasant and scenic way to enter Detroit from Canada than the Ambassador Bridge, but it empties out on E. Jefferson at the foot of Randolph Street, next to the Renaissance Center (fare $1.50 per car). The tunnel can get jammed with traffic waiting to get through customs, so plan to pass through on a weekday morning or late at night. If you need local tourist information, swing around Jefferson to the Visitor Information Center (9:00 a.m. to 5:00 p.m., Monday to Friday, 313-567-1170), in Hart Plaza, in front of Ford Auditorium, just west of where you came out of the tunnel. There are 15-minute free parking spots there. (You also can get local information later at the information kiosk in the Jefferson Avenue lobby of RenCen.)

**What to See: Lock #3's Viewing Centre** on the **Welland Canal** in St. Catharines also has audiovisual and other displays. There's free parking and a snack bar. Two miles northwest of Lock #3 is picturesque Port Dalhousie at Lake Street, where the Welland Canal begins. **Port Dalhousie** is full of restored nineteenth-century buildings with quaint shops and restaurants.

St. Catharines is located in very scenic countryside, especially in early May when fruit orchards are blooming. Visit the **Royal Botanical Gardens Centre** where you can purchase a Visitor Guide from the Information Desk. Comprised of 2,700 acres, the RBG includes a 1,200-acre game preserve of marsh and woodland with 30 miles of trails running through it. The arboretum is famous for its lilacs—over 1,000 bushes blooming in May—and fields of irises in June. Open 9:00 a.m. to dusk. Parking at the Rock Gardens is $2.50. During the summer months, two restaurants in the RBG serve light meals.

The first-rate **Folk Art Festival**, Folk Art Multicultural Centre, 85 Church Street, is in late May, the **Royal Canadian Henley Rowing Regatta** is in early August, and the **Niagara Grape and Wine Festival** take place from mid- to late September. Keep these festivities in mind when planning your trip to Niagara. The **Tivoli Miniature World** is about eight miles north of St. Catharines reached on Prudhomme Boulevard from the QEW. More than 80 scale replicas of famous structures (the Egyptian Pyramids, St. Peter's Basilica, Acropolis of Athens, the Cathedral of Cologne, etc. ) are displayed. In summer, it is open daily from 9:00 a.m. to 10:00 p.m.; adults $6.25, children 5 to 12 $3.

**Stratford**, the highest city in Ontario, is the home of the world-famous **Stratford Shakespearean Festival**. For those who plan to attend a Stratford Festival performance, from the RBG take Highway 8 through Kitchener/ Waterloo to Stratford. On the Festival Stage, you'll see Shakespearean presentations; on the Avon Stage, operas, operettas, and contemporary drama and musicals; and regional showcases are on the Third Stage. You may find *Guys and Dolls* playing along with *Macbeth* and *Julius Caesar* and Eugene O'Neill's *Ah, Wilderness!* Festival Theatre Box Office, P.O. Box 520, Stratford, Ontario, N5A 6V2, (519) 273-1600.

En route to Leamington from Stratford or directly from Hamilton, at the junction of Highway 3 and Highway 76, in Eagle, stop at **Swains Greenhouses**, 3 ½ acres of tropical gardens and a garden restaurant with excellent coffee and homemade goodies. Farther on, Blenheim is a pleasant town in fruit orchid country where you can buy local pears, apples, and cherries. There are also many roadside stands on Route 3 as you drive from Leamington, "the tomato capital of Canada," to Windsor.

**Point Pelee** is the "hot spot" for bird-watching along the Lake Erie coast. Banners across the streets welcome birders in droves heading for Kopegaron Woods Conservation Area, Hillman Marsh Conservation Area, the Onion Fields, and especially Point Pelee National Park. To get to Point Pelee, take a left off Erie Street on Seacliffe Drive. Point Pelee, 6 miles south of town, is a sandspit of marsh, grass, trees, and vast numbers of birds. May 6 through 20 is spring bird-watching, and September through November is the fall season. Monarch butterflies migrate in mid-September. This is a major park with over 20 miles of hiking trails and 14 miles of beach. You can p>walk half a mile out into the marsh on a boardwalk and climb a 36-foot observation tower to watch birds and wildlife in the marsh. Canoes and bicycles can be rented in the park.</p>

**Pelee Island**, the largest island in Lake Erie, has ferry service at 9:00 a.m. and 6:00 p.m. from Leamington, returning at 7:00 a.m. and 4:00 p.m., June 12 through Labor day on the *M.V. Pelee Islander*, (519) 724-2115, toll-free in the 519 area at (800) 265-5683. Pelee Island may be best known for its pheasant hunting. The pheasants are brought to the island as chicks and raised for hunting, which takes place on the last Thursday and Friday in October and the first and second Thursday and Friday in November (and thus doesn't interfere with looking at fall foliage).

If you drive a little farther beyond Leamington to Kingsville on Route 18, at the Pelee Island Winery, (519) 733-6551, you can taste Riesling, Pinot Noir, and other wines from grapes grown on Pelee Island. In late March or late October to early November, you can see wild geese at the **Jack Miner Bird Sanctuary** in Kingsville.

**Food: The Leamington Dock Restaurant**, (519) 326-2697, at the end of Erie Street on the dock for the boat to Pelee Island, serves yellow perch, Lake Erie pickerel, and light fare, too, with a view of Lake Erie from its big picture window. For gourmet dining, let John Ingratta, the former general manager of the local Heinz factory, take care of you with old-fashioned Canadian hospitality and warmth. John bought the **Thirteen Russell** restaurant, (519) 326-8401, which is in a turn-of-the-century home (reputed to be the first in Leamington with indoor plumbing), and maintains the highest standard of cuisine. Chef Rafael's roast prime rib of beef and the Vitello alla Parmigiana are delicious.

# DETROIT

Visit one of the nation's foremost art museums, the
Detroit Institute of Arts. Board the People Mover and
enjoy views of the city center and its impressive art deco
office towers, the hustle and bustle of Greektown, Bricktown's nightclubs and bars, and the Detroit River. Enjoy
the gaudy opulence of the Fox Theater while seeing a top
live performance. Experience what the "New Detroit" is
all about at the developing riverfront east of the huge
RenCen, where new office buildings and apartment com-
plexes adjoin warehouses renovated into nightclubs and
restaurants.

## Suggested Schedule

| | |
|---|---|
| 8:30 a.m. | Leave Port Huron for Detroit. |
| 9:30 a.m. | Check into hotel in downtown Detroit. |
| 10:30 a.m. | Drive to the Detroit Institute of Arts (DIA). |
| 1:00 p.m. | Lunch at the DIA. |
| 2:00 p.m. | People Mover and Downtown Trolley touring. |
| 3:00 p.m. | Greektown and Bricktown touring. |
| 6:00 p.m. | Dinner in Greektown. |
| 7:45 p.m. | Drive to the Fox Theater or entertainment in Rivertown. |

**Travel Route: Port Huron to Detroit (45 miles)**
From Port Huron, take I-94 to I-75 to I-375 in Detroit
(45 miles), and exit on Jefferson Avenue west to the Day's
Inn at Michigan Avenue and Washington Boulevard. Or
drive east to Blanche House B&B on Parkview Drive, a
little over one mile east of the Belle Isle Bridge on the
Belle Isle side of Waterworks Park. To get from downtown to the Detroit Institute of Arts, take I-75 to the
Warren exit, exit west on Warren to Woodward, and turn
left toward Wayne State University and the Cultural Center complex, or exit I-94 at John R/Woodward exit and

proceed south on John R four blocks to Farnsworth. Return to the Day's Inn or other downtown parking (see below), and use the Detroit People Mover for the rest of the afternoon until the drive this evening to the Fox Theater.

**Getting Around**
The **Detroit People Mover**, a monorail system, costs only 50 cents to cover a nearly 3-mile loop around down-town. It stops at 12 well-patrolled stations, where you'll see exceptional local art in the entryways and on the plat-forms. Be sure to pick up a copy of *Art in the Stations*, which pinpoints all of the stations and depicts examples of the outstanding artwork in each station. The People Mover is uncrowded because one departs every 3 to 4 minutes and because far fewer people ride the system than originally projected.

For direct access to the People Mover, park at the Millender Center, which includes the Omni Hotel and Atrium Retail Stores, across the street from RenCen. You can also park in the less expensive, but less convenient "A" transient lot off Beaubien east of RenCen, or in the Ford Auditorium Garage. The People Mover runs Monday through Thursday 7:00 a.m. to 11 p.m., Friday 7:00 a.m. to midnight, Saturday 9:00 a.m. to midnight, Sunday noon to 8:00 p.m. The 15-minute trip provides excellent views of the city and the river, especially as the route swings around Joe Louis Arena. Go around the loop for one full sightseeing trip, then get off at **Bricktown Station** (Beaubien at Fort). Bricktown's warehouses and storefronts have been converted into restaurants, shops, nightclubs, and galleries.

On a nice day, if you want to see elegant old office buildings from an antique trolley, perhaps from an open upper deck, instead of using the People Mover to return to RenCen from **Grand Circus Park**, take the **Down-town Trolley** that follows Washington Boulevard and Jefferson between Grand Circus Park and Hart Plaza. Trolleys depart at 15-minute intervals on weekdays 7:00 a.m.

to 6:00 p.m. and weekends 10:00 a.m. to 6:00 p.m., for a
45 cent fare. Look for 1920s financial center architectural gems by architect Wirt Rowland, at the corners of
Griswold, Congress, and Fort. Don't miss the Guardian,
Buhl, Ford, and Penobscot buildings, easily accessible
from the Financial District Station on the People Mover.

**Detroit**
The village, town, and city of Detroit had almost two
hundred years of history as a fur trading, lumbering,
transportation, whitefish shipping, and boat and railroad
car building center before the boom years of automobile
production. The city that you see today was largely
created by auto barons in the 1910s and 1920s. By 1910,
Henry Ford, the Dodge brothers, and other aggressive
local businessmen had put Detroit ahead of 175 other
U.S. cities in making automobiles. Starting in 1900, the
population almost doubled every decade until 1930, as
the city turned out half of the world's cars.

   Blacks moved to the city from the South in response to
labor shortages during World War I and World War II.
After explosive wartime and postwar production years,
the auto factories moved to the suburbs, and the population started to decline. Downtown shops, department
stores, hotels, and office buildings closed, while federal,
state, and local funds were poured into riverfront and
downtown projects like Millender Center, Harbortown,
River Place, The Lofts at Rivertown, and Jeffersonian,
Indian Village, and Riverfront apartments.

   The meeting places of locals and visitors in Detroit
today are the **Renaissance Center** (RenCen) and the
adjoining **Hart Plaza**. RenCen includes the world's
tallest hotel, the 73-story Westin. RenCen's tiers of atrium
shopping are a disappointment for shoppers, but for a
view of the Detroit River from Lake St. Clair nearly to
Lake Erie, it is worth buying a snack at the revolving
**Summit Steak House** on the hotel's 72nd floor. The
Summit Observation Deck on the 73rd floor of the hotel
charges a $3 admission fee.

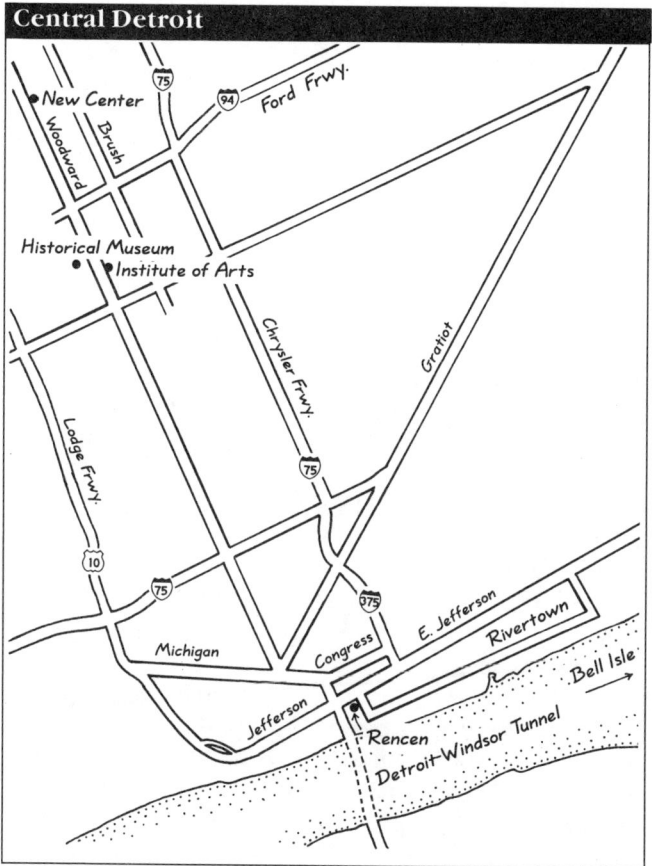

**Central Detroit**

**Hart Plaza**, at the foot of Woodward Avenue, adjoining the RenCen, is the scene of summer activity like the weekly ethnic festivals; the Downtown Hoedown country music fest in mid-May; and the Montreux-Detroit Jazz Festival over Labor Day weekend. At the river are anchored the *Star of Detroit* cruise boat, with lunches, dinners, and sightseeing cruises, and the *Lansdowne*, an old railroad ferry turned into a floating restaurant. (Unfortunately, **Ford Hall** is slated to be demolished and replaced by a 40-story bank-office structure, which also means that Hart Plaza will be afflicted by construction activity for several years.)

## Sightseeing Highlights

▲▲▲ **Detroit Institute of Arts**—Since it charges no admission, this great museum continuously faces financial problems that force it to close on Mondays and Tuesdays. The museum is vast and labyrinthine. Guided tours Wednesday through Saturday at 12:15 p.m. and Sunday at 1:00 p.m. and 2:30 p.m. are helpful for orientation to the exhibits that span Mesopotamian to American, Italian Renaissance, Dutch-Flemish, and German expressionist art. Have lunch in Kresge Court, a courtyard dining area reminiscent of the Bargello Palace in Florence, or in La Palette. Visit the museum shop for books, posters, slides, and gift items. 5200 Woodward Avenue, (313) 833-7900, Wednesday through Sunday 9:30 a.m. to 5:30 p.m. Donations are welcome—and needed!

▲ **Detroit Historical Museum**—Across the street from the DIA, the museum has a unique display in its basement of nighttime scenes of nineteenth-century Detroit commercial street fronts, built to three-quarters scale along cobblestone and brick streets. 5401 Woodward Avenue (across from the DIA); 9:30 a.m. to 5:00 p.m. Wednesday through Sunday; (313) 833-1605.

▲ **Trappers Alley**—In Greektown, on Beaubien between Lafayette and Monroe, is a late-nineteenth-century tannery converted into a well-designed four-level shopping center that would be more festive (like Faneuil Hall in Boston) if the specialty stores and restaurants were more interesting.

▲▲▲ **The Fox Theater**—Recently restored by Mike Ilitch, owner of Caesar's Pizza and the Detroit Red Wings, to its former incredible grandeur, the theater is on Woodward, three blocks north of Grand Circus Park and the Grand Circus Park Station of the People Mover. If you attend a show there, you will see its eclectic Asian interior with a six-story lobby that looks and feels more like an exquisite Hindu temple. The Grand Circus Park Station is at the David Whitney Building, with rich marble and wood, a magnificent atrium, galleries, restaurants, and shops.

▲▲ **Rivertown**—A four-block area between Jefferson and the river east of RenCen toward Belle Isle, Rivertown consists of old warehouses and factories that are gradually being transformed into nightlife hot spots. The Soup Kitchen Saloon blues and jazz club, 1585 Franklin at Orleans, (313) 299-2643, has national acts like John Hammond and Albert Collins as well as outstanding local acts like Uncle Jessie White. Open Tuesday through Saturday, 7:30 p.m. to 2:00 a.m.; Sunday, 7:00 p.m. to midnight; cover $4 to $9 on weekends, The Soup Kitchen is tame entertainment compared with Taboo, 1940 Woodbridge, (313) 567-6140, and the Rhinoceros, 265 Riopelle, (313) 259-1374. In Rivertown's **Stroh River Place**, nearly 2 miles from downtown out East Jefferson to the foot of Joseph Campeau, in the former 30-acre headquarters and manufacturing site of Parke Davis pharmaceuticals, the Rattlesnake Club, (313) 567-4400, serves shrimp, crab, and salmon cakes as their specialty on a wonderful outdoor patio and excellent food of every description at reasonable prices. Open Monday through Thursday 11:30 a.m. to 11:00 p.m., Friday and Saturday until 1:00 a.m. Three riverfront parks in Rivertown—St. Aubin; Chene, with its excellent summer arts festival and outdoor amphitheater; and Mt. Elliott, designed as a historical interpretive center—one day will be linked by pedestrian and bicycle paths.

▲ **Belle Isle**—Attracting swarms of visitors day and night, especially evenings and weekends during warm weather, Belle Isle is the largest urban park in the United States. It's well patrolled by police and safe for outings. This beautiful park offers great panoramic views of Detroit, the river, and Canada; the small but exceptional Belle Isle Zoo, with a ¾-mile-long elevated walkway from which to view 160 species of animals in naturalistic settings; the nation's oldest freshwater aquarium and still one of the most beautifully and magically designed (by Albert Kahn) including a 2,800-gallon tank of major groups of Great Lakes fish; the Dossin Great Lakes Museum featuring artwork and artifacts salvaged from shipwrecks, the beautifully carved interior of the 1912 steamer, the *City of Detroit*, and models of Great Lakes ships; excellent fishing for silver bass, blue gill, perch, and other fish; canals for canoeing the length of the island; and a nature center with trails and deer in its forests.

▲ **New Center One**—Three miles north of downtown, New Center One includes the GM Building, the St. Regis Hotel, the trapezoid-shaped New Center One, the Albert Kahn Building, and the magnificently ornate Fisher Building, W. Grand Boulevard at 2nd Avenue, capped by its famous Golden Tower, perhaps the world's most beautiful office building. These structures are connected by skywalks. Visit the Detroit Gallery of Contemporary Crafts, (313) 873-7888, in the main lobby of the Fisher Building and also look at the building's stunning interior arcade. This area includes the Fisher Theater, which stages Broadway plays and has marvelous acoustics, and the Attic Theater, 7339 3rd Avenue, (313) 875-8284, producing off-Broadway plays.

▲ **Historic Homes of the Auto Barons**—Visit one of four opulent estates built with the wealth of the Detroit auto empires. For the Fisher Mansion in Detroit, see below. For the Henry Ford Estate, Fair Lane, see Day 20. The Edsel and Eleanor Ford House, in Grosse Pointe Shores, is an elegant Cotswold-style mansion on 62 beautiful acres. To reach it, take Lake Shore Road to I-94, get off at the 9 Mile Road exit, follow 9 Mile to Jefferson Avenue, turn right on Jefferson, and follow until once again it becomes Lake Shore Road. The entrance is on the left, just past the Grosse Pointe border at 1100 Lake Shore Road, (313) 884-4222. Open Monday through Friday, 9:00 a.m. to 7:30 p.m.; Saturday and Sunday, 9 a.m. to noon and 5:00 to 8:00 p.m.

And there's the Matilda Dodge Wilson Estate, Meadow Brook Hall, at Oakland University in Rochester, one of the grandest estates in the world. It cost $4 million in 1929 and is full of priceless art treasures. Meadow Brook Hall is northeast of Pontiac off I-75, well off the path of this itinerary.

▲ **Fisher Mansion**—One of the most lavish and amazingly fanciful residences of the ultra rich in the United States, this mansion was created by Lawrence P. Fisher, founder of the Fisher Body Company. It has been restored by one of the most improbable couples imaginable: Brush Ford, the great-grandson of Henry Ford, and Elisabeth Reuther, daughter of the late Walter Reuther, former head of the United Auto Workers. Both Ford and Reuther are Hare Krishna converts and have established the Bhaktivedanta Cultural Center at the mansion. Completed in 1927, the mansion features ornate stone and marble work, exquisite European handcrafted stained glass windows, art deco tile, and spectacular chandeliers. The center operates one of the Midwest's best vegetarian restaurants, **Govinda's** (313) 331-6740, open only on the weekends. To reach the mansion, take I-94 to the Conner Avenue exit, drive on Conner south to Jefferson, go two stoplights to Dickerson, and turn right. Follow Dickerson until it becomes Lenox. 383 Lenox, (313) 331-6740. Open Friday, Saturday, and Sunday year-round from noon to 9:00 p.m. Tours are on Friday and Saturday at 12:30, 2:00, 3:30, and 6:00 p.m.; Sunday at noon, 1:30, 3:00, and 6:00 p.m. Admission is $4.

▲ **Boblo Island**—An amusement park since 1898, 272-acre Boblo will satisfy almost every thrill-seeker. The 75 rides are highlighted by a roller-coaster trip through a dark, enclosed chamber. Water-skiing shows and other entertainment in the Carousel Theatre are part of the ticket price. The island also is perfect for bicycle riding. Take I-75 south of the Ambassador Bridge to the Clark Avenue exit (47A), then go two blocks toward the river to the Boblo Dock, where there's plentiful parking. From here, it's a 1-hour, 10-minute boat ride on the top deck of

one of the old Boblo steamers, listed in the National
Historic Registry. The boat trip and all rides cost $15.95
for ages 7 to 50, $13.51 for ages 51 and over, and $9.95
for ages 3 to 6. Detroit departures are at 9:30 and 10:30 a.m.,
and in summer months also at 1:30 and 3:30 p.m., with
hourly return trips after 3:30 until 8:30 p.m. For the sailing schedule, call (313) 843-0700. There's also a moonlight cruise from 11:00 p.m. to 1:00 a.m. Fridays and
Saturdays for $10.95.

## Lodging
The **Day's Inn** at Michigan Avenue and Washington
Boulevard, (313) 965-4646 or (800) 325-2525, is about as
central as you can get, with good views of the Detroit
River, and free breakfast for $55 single and $65 double.
B&B enthusiasts will appreciate the restored turn-of-the-
century **Blanche House Bed & Breakfast**, (313) 822-7090,
506 Parkview Drive, a little over 1 mile east of the Belle
Isle Bridge on the Belle Isle side of Waterworks Park and
only a block from the river. Rooms with antique furnish-
ings, beautifully carved woodwork, and private baths,
and a suite with a hot tub, rent for $65 to $110. Next door
to this 1905 Colonial Revival in the historic Berry Sub-
division, Mary Jean and Sean Shannon are converting a
former boys' school into an expansion of their B&B.

## Camping
If you plan to camp outside Detroit, from Flint take U.S.
23 (instead of I-75 south) all the way to Highway 59
(Highland Road), 10 miles east to the **Highland State
Recreation Area**. At Highland, 5200 E. Highland Road,
Milford, MI 48042, (313) 887-5135, the Dodge #10 campground offers 39 shaded sites with plenty of privacy but
no electricity or showers. Or turn right (south) off Highway 59 at Milford Road, just before the Highland State
Recreation Area, and follow Milford, Commerce, Duck,
and Wixom roads another 10 miles to **Proud Lake
Recreation Area**, 3500 Wixom Road, Milford, MI
48042, (313) 685-2433. A chain of lakes around the Hut-

ton River and thousands of acres of beautiful woodlands surround 130 modern campsites on the crest of a hill at Proud Lake. The sites have electricity and showers but are small and lack shade and privacy. The setting makes the campground worthwhile.

**Food**
**Greektown** has six Greek restaurants on Monroe Street between St. Antoine and Beaubien, as well as other Greek shops, bakeries, grocery stores, and coffeehouses that bustle with activity until at least 2:00 a.m. all week long. Check out the smells of fresh bread, cheeses, olives, and pastries in the **Athens** or **Monroe Grocery and Bakery** next door to each other on Monroe and the **Stemma Bakery** across the street. More elegant and delicious pastries and cakes are on the other side of Trappers Alley (see Sightseeing Highlights, above) at **Susan Hoffmann Pastries**, 1219 St. Antoine, 7:30 a.m. to 6:00 p.m. It's next to the city parking structure where you can park (from Monroe Street) to visit Greektown if you decide not to take the People Mover.

**The Blue Nile**, (313) 964-6699, on the second floor of Trappers Alley, serves Ethiopian dinners from 5:00 to 10:00 p.m. daily, worth pairing with an evening at the Fox Theater. If you haven't eaten Ethiopian-style before, you're in for an experience: low chairs with goatskin cushions are set next to communal platters containing lamb, chicken, and beef dishes eaten with fresh bread instead of silverware. All-you-can-eat meat or vegetarian feasts cost $10.90 to $13.90.

Before leaving the Cultural Center and Wayne State campus area, have dinner at **Traffic Jam & Snug**, 511 W. Canfield, (313) 831-9470. Besides the eclectic menu, it's noted for award-winning cheeses, made on the premises, wonderful bread, good value in wines, a micro-brewery, and great desserts.

Coney Island hot dogs at the **American Coney Island** ($1.30 with chili, cheese 25 cents extra) have been

a Detroit institution for more than 75 years at 115 W.
Michigan, between Griswald and Shelby. It's open 24
hours a day, seven days a week. If you want to eat with a
cross section of Detroit's citizens anytime of day, it's
either here or next door at the **Lafayette Coney Island**.
Both places serve about 15 varieties of beer.

**Carl's Chop House**, 3020 Grand River, (313)
833-0700, Monday through Saturday 11:30 a.m. to midnight, Sunday 2:00 to 10:00 p.m., is Detroit's most popular and one of its oldest steak and prime rib houses. It's
probably also the noisiest, which has to be part of its
attraction.

**The Whitney**, 221 Woodward, (313) 832-5700, a
restored masterpiece of architecture and decor, serves
excellent and expensive food. Don't hesitate to order just
soup and salad or dessert and coffee to enjoy the
environment.

## DEARBORN

The **Henry Ford Estate, Fair Lane**, is about five minutes away from the famed **Henry Ford Museum** and **Greenfield Village**, which Ford founded. Stroll through the rooms where the Fords entertained many of the world's most influential people, and see a great example of landscape art in the vast gardens and meadows. At the museum and village, visit the **Wright Brothers' Cycle Shop, Thomas Edison's laboratory** from Menlo Park, and 93 acres packed with American history that you won't see anywhere else. Truly a celebration of Main Street U.S.A., this grouping of historic buildings in Greenfield Village spans from the 1600s to present times. The village and Henry Ford Museum make up the Edison Institute.

### Suggested Schedule

| | |
|---|---|
| 8:00 a.m. | Breakfast in Detroit and check-out. |
| 9:00 a.m. | Drive to Dearborn. |
| 10:00 a.m. | Tour the Henry Ford Estate. |
| 12:00 noon | Lunch at the Pool Restaurant. |
| 1:00 p.m. | Leave for Henry Ford Museum and Greenfield Village. |
| 1:30 p.m. | Tour Henry Ford Museum and Greenfield Village. |
| 5:00 p.m. | Leave and check into lodgings, or drive to camping near Ann Arbor. |
| 6:30 p.m. | Evening in Dearborn or at campground. |

**Travel Route: Detroit to Dearborn (15 miles)**
To get to the first stop at the Henry Ford Estate, head west from Detroit on I-94 for 15 miles to Highway 12, Michigan Avenue. Head west on Michigan Avenue for three miles, then right on Evergreen between Michigan Avenue and Ford Road, and park at the visitor center. Return to Michigan Avenue, turn right and head to West Dearborn.

In less than a mile turn left (south) onto Oakwood Boulevard and left again in ¼ mile into the museum and village
parking lot. In Dearborn, my suggested accommodations
are just around the corner from the Henry Ford
Museum—take a right on Michigan Avenue. For camping
near Ann Arbor, see directions to the two suggested
camping choices below.

**Dearborn and Henry Ford**
The city of Dearborn is the product of Henry Ford, who
was born at the corner of Greenfield and Ford roads.
After moving back from Detroit in 1916, he brought his
company here and built the world's largest automobile
factory, the Rouge Plant. Ford did things in a big way,
such as purchasing six square miles between Dearborn
and Springwells. He preserved much of the Rouge River
area as parkland. In this area, just south of Michigan Avenue, he created Greenfield Village and the Henry Ford
Museum to depict the history of America's technological
evolution and its impact on Americans in all walks of life.

**Sightseeing Highlights**
▲▲▲ **Henry Ford Estate (Fair Lane)**—This 56-room
estate on the banks of the Rouge River is a very strange
blend of medieval Scottish baronial castle and Frank
Lloyd Wright. Much more of Ford's down-to-earth style
is evident in the huge hydroelectric power plant, connected to the mansion by a tunnel, that he created with
his brilliant friend, Thomas Edison. About half of the 1½ -
hour tour of the estate is devoted to the power plant and
its remarkable 110-kilowatt electric system.
    The surrounding 1,600 acres include a wonderful
meadow leading to a pond hidden in the woods, a
delightful cascade, and terraced paths along the river.
Walk the beautiful footpaths and trails (bring binoculars
for bird-watching), stroll in the rose garden where more
than 10,000 rose plants grow, have a light lunch at The
Pool restaurant (see Food, below), and visit the Fair Lane
Gift Shop for a souvenir. Guided tours for a nominal fee

leave on the hour from 10:00 a.m. to 3:00 p.m. (except at noon). 4901 Evergreen, (313) 593-5590, open sunrise to sunset daily. Admission is $2 grounds and $6 house; $5 seniors and children 6 to 12.

▲▲▲ **The Henry Ford Museum and Greenfield Village**—The largest and probably the most enjoyable indoor-outdoor museum in the United States, the Henry Ford Museum documents ordinary life in this country and how it was transformed by technology in the late nineteenth and early twentieth centuries. Village highlights include Ford's own birthplace, a Greek Revival farmhouse built in 1861; the Menlo Park Compound, Thomas Edison's 1880 laboratories; the Wright Cycle Shop, the birthplace of aviation; and the exhibit "The Automobile in American Life." The latter will take you back to a 1946 diner, a 1950s drive-in theater with a feature film, and a 1960s motel room. You can travel through Greenfield Village in a nineteenth-century train or horse-drawn carriage, with a stop at the old Eagle Tavern for food and drink. You can also watch demonstrations of early trades, like glassblowing, weaving, and pottery making, and get a feel for life on the farm where Harvey Firestone was born.

The Henry Ford Museum has an amazing collection of nineteenth-century farm and kitchen implements, tractors, airplanes, cars, and old steam engines, as well as a bewildering collection of other displays and theme exhibits. Combined admission to the museum and village is $18 for adults and $8 for children 5 to 12 for two days, and $10.50 for adults and $5.25 for children for one day. Both facilities are open 9:00 a.m. to 5:00 p.m. daily. Check on special weekends and exhibits such as live swing music of the '30s and '40s, a fashion show from yesteryear, an antiques show with dealers from across the country, a parade of more than 100 vintage cars, and holiday events. Seeing just half of Greenfield Village will take at least three hours and the museum another three hours.

▲ **Commandant's Quarters/Dearborn Historical Museum**—These buildings at 21950 Michigan Avenue at Monroe Boulevard in downtown West Dearborn, (313)

565-3000, are what is left of an arsenal constructed in Dearborn over 150 years ago. A combination of excellent restoration work, period rooms, and a fine library available to the public make this one of the better local museums in the state. The Museum Exhibit Annex, 915 Brady Street (attached to the Fairlane Inn, see below), displays an assortment of blacksmithing, carpentry, and saddlery artifacts.

## Lodging

In Dearborn, **The Fairlane Inn**, 21430 Michigan Avenue, (313) 565-0800, overlooking the Rouge River, features quiet rooms in rear buildings that overlook wooded back acres. It is perfectly located for touring local attractions and costs only $45 to $65 for singles and doubles with queen or double beds and a continental breakfast. The inn is just two minutes away from the Oakwood Boulevard turnoff to Greenfield Village, and the Ford estate is just up the road. The Dearborn Historical Museum Exhibit Annex is attached to a wall of the inn. The Chicago Roadhouse next door offers a 20 percent discount to inn guests on very good meals and drinks. One of the best features of the inn is that it's a short walk from **Ford Field**, where you can jog or take a brisk walk away from traffic in the morning or evening. On the second weekend in June, an all-day re-creation of a semblance of the French and Indian War ("Rendezvous on the Rouge") takes place on Ford Field. The event includes mock-serious ceremonies, fun, fanfare, and a heritage fair where antiques, collectibles, handcrafts, and goodies are sold.

The nearby **Village Inn of Dearborn**, 21725 Michigan Avenue, (313) 565-8511, is smaller and less luxurious than the Fairlane Inn but still a perfectly adequate motel, with $40 to $48 singles and doubles.

## Camping

Both of these campgrounds are about 60 miles and a little over an hour from Dearborn. If you check in tonight at the **Pinckney Recreation Area**, 8555 Silver Hill, Route 1, Pinckney, MI 48169, (313) 426-4913, you can stay for two nights, leaving on Day 22. Pinckney covers 10,000 acres and contains 220 modern campsites with electricity and showers and 35 rustic ones that are secluded, private, and tree-shaded. Enjoy Bruin Lake and more than a dozen other lakes, plus 60 miles of hiking trails. Take I-94 west to U.S. 23. Six miles north of Ann Arbor, at Exit 49, drive west on North Territorial Road for about 7 miles.

A second excellent camping choice is to drive down I-94 past Ann Arbor and Chelsea to Exit 147 north, to Route 147, where you'll see signs for **Waterloo Recreation Area**. Take a right on Rte. 147. The 20,000-acre Waterloo Recreation Area, 16345 McLure Rd., Chelsea, MI 48118, (313) 475-8307, has 380 modern and 50 rustic campsites. For a beautiful campground with modern conveniences, head for the Portage Lake Unit with 194 units. For more privacy, try the Sugarloaf Campground's 184 units. The largest park in the Lower Peninsula, Waterloo has dozens of fishing lakes, a swimming beach, a beautiful nature preserve for sandhill cranes (Haehnle Audubon Sanctuary), 8 nature trails, and other facilities.

**Food**
**The Pool** at the Henry Ford Estate initially was the mansion's swimming pool. A variety of tasty sandwiches is served for under $5, soup and salad bar for less, between 11:00 a.m. and 2:00 p.m.

**Giovanni's**, 330 S. Oakwood in Dearborn, just south of the Ford Rouge, reached by the Oakwood Exit off I-94, is recommended for outstanding homemade pasta, especially spinach ravioli filled with veal and sweet onions over spinach fettucine.

For Sunday brunch or a splurge dinner, try **The Early American Room** at the **Dearborn Inn**, 20301 Oakwood, across from Greenfield Village, (313) 271-2700. Reservations are essential.

## Entertainment
**Moby Dick Lounge**, 5452 Shaefer, Dearborn, (313) 581-3650, sees some of Detroit's finest blues acts on Friday and Saturday, starting at 8:30 p.m.

# ANN ARBOR

A delightful place for strolling and people-watching at sidewalk cafes, Ann Arbor offers visitors outstanding museums, theater, entertainment, and restaurants thanks to the presence of the University of Michigan. From the refurbished streetscape on Main Street, walk to historic Kerrytown for lunch. See the famous Farmers Market in action, then return to town on Liberty and State streets to enjoy bookstore browsing and university attractions. Time your visit for July's Summer Festival, art fairs, and Antiques Market.

## Suggested Schedule

| | |
|---|---|
| 8:30 a.m. | Breakfast, check-out, and drive to Ann Arbor. |
| 10:30 a.m. | Arrive in downtown Ann Arbor, park and begin walking tour down E. Liberty. |
| 11:00 a.m. | Main Street to Kerrytown. |
| 12:00 noon | Lunch in Kerrytown. |
| 1:00 p.m. | Walk south on Fifth Avenue to E. Liberty, east to S. State. |
| 1:15 p.m. | Visit Hands-on Museum. |
| 2:15 p.m. | Tour the University of Michigan campus. |
| 4:30 p.m. | State Street strolling and browsing. |
| 6:00 p.m. | Check in and get ready for dinner. |
| 7:00 p.m. | Dinner. |
| 8:30 p.m. | Evening entertainment. |

**Travel Route: Dearborn to Ann Arbor (28 miles)**

From Dearborn, drive east on Oakwood Boulevard to the Southfield Freeway, which shortly joins I-94 west. It's 28 miles to Ann Arbor. In Ann Arbor, turn off I-94 on State Street (don't turn north on BR/94). Turn on E. Liberty and then on Thompson to the parking garage in the middle of the block, or turn left on S. Fifth Avenue to park behind the Ann Arbor Public Library. Then you can walk

east on Liberty to Main Street, then north on Main to Kerrytown and back to town on N. Fifth, past the Hands-on
Museum. Or, from your parking spot, walk west on Liberty to S. State Street and the University of Michigan
Campus.

## Sightseeing Highlights
**▲▲▲ Ann Arbor's downtown and Kerrytown**—
You'll find more shops, restaurants, bookstores, and
historical places to visit in central Ann Arbor than in any
other place of its size in the Great Lakes. The Ann Arbor
Summer Festival, art fairs, and the Antiques Market, all
in July, make it an especially good month for visitors. To
be sure you're not missing the best happenings, contact
the very helpful Ann Arbor Convention and Visitors
Bureau, 211 East Huron, Ste. 6, Ann Arbor, MI 48104, (313)
995-7281, for information on upcoming events, and ask
for a copy of the visitor's guide.

**▲▲ Main Street and Liberty Street**—Congratulations
to Ann Arbor for the improvements to these principal
streets. New light poles and lighting with a soft opaque
glow, plantings, sidewalk improvements, and flourishing
outdoor cafes are what city life should be about.

**▲▲ Kerrytown**—More than 30 shops and restaurants in
three restored historic buildings surround a pleasant
courtyard and are framed by the Ann Arbor Farmers Market.
In addition to fish, produce, and natural food stores, the
Kerrytown Bistro and Moveable Feast's Kerrytown Shop
have all the delicious food you could possibly want midday or evening. The Treasure Mart will make you wish
you had a van to haul away bargain collectibles, furnish-
ings, and the like from this resale shop. Open Tuesday
through Thursday 9:00 a.m. to 5:30 p.m.; Monday and
Friday until 8:30 p.m.; and Saturday 9:00 a.m. to 5:30 p.m.

**▲▲ The Farmers Market**—Located between Detroit
and N. Fourth. It is easy to park near the market on weekdays. On Saturday mornings, however, you must park
several blocks away, for example, just west of Main in the
Ashley-Ann parking structure.

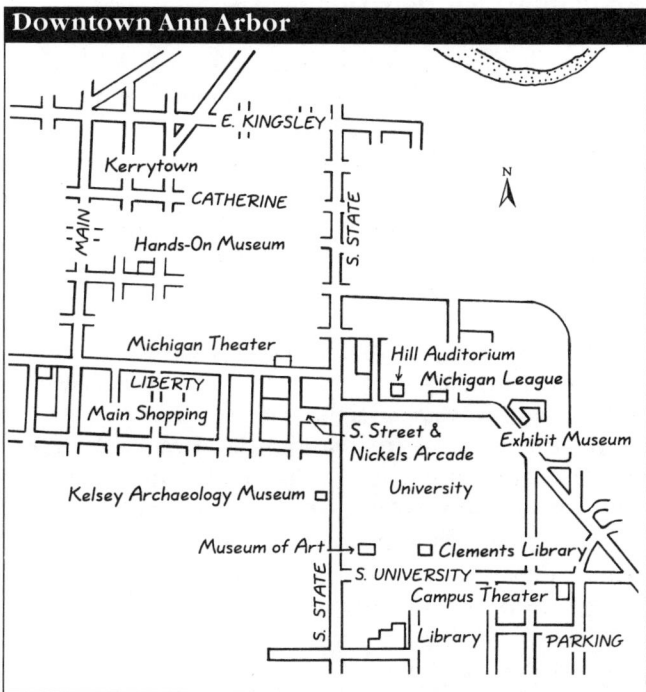

Downtown Ann Arbor

▲▲ **The Hands-on Museum**—Housed in a circa 1879 fire station, next door to the Ann Arbor Convention and Visitors Bureau and across from City Hall, the museum, 219 East Huron, (313) 995-KIDS, focuses on learning by doing and connects science with art. Most of the 150 exhibits on four floors are fascinating, like the reflection hologram microscope and the hot air balloon powered by toasters. The computer room has 14 computers with educational game software. Certainly every family traveling together in southeastern Michigan should plan to spend a few hours connecting physics, math, art, robotics, and games at the museum. Open Tuesday through Friday 10:00 a.m. to 5:30 p.m., Saturday 10:00 a.m. to 5:00 p.m., and Sunday 1:00 to 5:00 p.m. Adults $3, children $2, and families a maximum of $7.50.

▲▲ **State Street and vicinity**—A stroll on State between Liberty and the university campus takes you past wonderful Borders Book Shop and, on the other side of the street, the Nickels Arcade running under a glass enclosure to Maynard Street.

▲▲ **The Kelsey Museum of Archaeology**—Located across from Angell Hall, this architectural gem contains an exceptional collection of ancient Greek, Egyptian, Roman, and Near Eastern artifacts. Open Monday to Friday 9:00 a.m. to 4:00 p.m., Saturday and Sunday 1:00 to 4:00 p.m.

▲ **The University of Michigan campus**—The institution covers 40 acres bounded by State and North, East, and South University. Of sightseeing interest on North University, one block from State, is the Michigan League building, which houses the Lydia Mendelssohn Theater. The U-M Exhibit Museum on Geddes has one of the world's foremost collections of natural science exhibits, a planetarium, which operates on weekends, and an excellent gift shop. Open Tuesday through Saturday 9:00 a.m. to 5:00 p.m., Sunday 1:00 to 5:00 p.m. Past neoclassic Angell Hall, start your tour at S. University with the University of Michigan Museum of Art. Open September through May, Tuesday through Friday 10:00 a.m. to 4:00 p.m., Saturday and Sunday 1:00 to 5:00 p.m.; June through August, Tuesday through Friday 11:00 a.m. to 4:00 p.m., Saturday and Sunday 1:00 to 5:00 p.m. Its collections are strong in many areas, like twentieth-century British and American sculpture. Next door is Albert Kahn's illustrious Clements Library of early American history; across the street, the picturesque Law Quadrangle; and across State, the Michigan Union.

## Lodging
**The Red Roof Inn**, (313) 996-5800 or (800) 843-7663, on U.S. 23 at Plymouth Road (Exit 41), four miles northeast of downtown, ranges from $39.95 to $51.95. For the price, this is the best hotel/motel value in the area. (The

walls of Red Roof Inns are known for good sound insulation.)

For a special B&B experience, try the **Reynolds House at Stonefield Farm**, 5259 West Ellsworth Road, (313) 995-0301, a cottage on 10 acres of rolling farmland, with 3 bedrooms, one bath, living room, and kitchen. Mary Reynolds serves an excellent full breakfast in the main house or on the sun deck in good weather ($60).

**Camping** (See Day 20)

**Food**

Part of the reason for being in Ann Arbor is to experience the cheeses, olives, smoked fish, and other delights at **Zingerman's Deli**, 442 Detroit, in Kerrytown. These delicacies are displayed with such verve they practically dare shoppers to try them. If you've never witnessed a feta cheese olympiad (pitting Greek against Bulgarian fetas), head for the Zing and get in line. Appropriately in a university town, Zingerman's distributes educational literature on smoked fish and gives gastronomical quizzes on smoked nova, sturgeon, whitefish, chubs (fatter, sweeter, and smokier than whitefish), and trout (imported by Zing from Ducktrap River Farms in Maine, no less!).

With Zingerman's around, it's almost sacrilegious to speak of lunch at **Amadeus**, 122 E. Washington, (313) 665-8767, but the frantic daily jam at the Zing may not appeal to everyone. Central European (i.e., Polish) and Austrian food is not everyone's midday fare, but pierogi (stuffed dumplings) definitely let you know that you've had lunch.

Kerrytown's quintessential culinary contribution to Ann Arbor just may be the **Kerrytown Bistro**, at 415 N. Fifth Avenue, (313) 994-6424: brick walls, wooden tables and benches, soft jazz, an excellent, relatively inexpensive selection of wines, and good spirits.

**Gratzi** (good guess, it's Italian), trattoria-style complete with strolling accordion player, is the liveliest place in town. Located in a huge old theater, Gratzi serves some of the best light Italian food at the price outside of Chicago. 326 S. Main, (313) 663-5555.

**Gandy Dancer**, 401 Depot, (313) 769-0592, in Ann Arbor's original railroad station, with a 15- to 20-foot ceiling, serves grilled, poached, or blackened fish specialties.

**Seva**, 314 Liberty Street, (313) 662-1111, deserves recognition as Ann Arbor's best inexpensive restaurant, serving vegetarian dishes based on Mexican, Italian, and Oriental cuisines.

**Entertainment**
**Bird of Paradise**, 207 S. Ashley, (313) 662-8310, re-creates a classic jazz club in a storefront where you can hear straight-ahead jazz by local musicians like the Ron Brooks Trio, Thursday through Saturday nights. Veteran bassist Ron Brooks gets credit for bringing this club to life and recently giving it yet another face lift.

**The Michigan Theater**, home of the Ann Arbor Symphony, sponsors a series of concerts, dramas, films, and other entertainment for adults and children, (313) 668-8480. Also check the program offerings of the **University of Michigan School of Music**, (313) 763-0965. There are folk offerings almost every night at **The Ark** (no phone), avant-garde plays at the **Performance Network**, (313) 663-0681, and musical offerings at the **Kerrytown Concert House**.

You might choose to plan your visit at the time of the **Ann Arbor Summer Festival**, which runs from around June 23 through July 15 and presents a fabulous schedule of dance, music, and theater events. In 1990, the festival included Pilobolus Dance Theatre, Emmylou Harris, Etta James, River City Brass Band, Chick Corea, and plays at the Michigan Theatre, such as *Swimming to Cambodia* and the *Anastasia Game* at the Lydia Mendelssohn Theatre.

For four days in the third week of July, Ann Arbor has a trio of art fairs—the **Ann Arbor Street Art Fair**, the

**State Street Art Fair**, and the **Summer Art Fair**—exhibiting juried work of hundreds of artists, and demonstrations of their work in all media. Jazz, classical, and folk musicians perform on stages around downtown. Musicians, mimes, and street entertainers are everywhere. Ethnic entertainment spans the globe, literally hundreds of children from toddlers to teenagers have places to exercise their artistic skills, and restaurants and stores have their best cuisine ready for shoulder-to-shoulder crowds.

**Ann Arbor Antiques Market** at the Washtenaw County Fairgrounds has been happening for more than 22 years on the third Sunday of each month (and the second Sunday of November) starting in April and ending in mid-November. More than 350 antique dealers offer deals on some of the best antiques you'll find anywhere, from chandeliers to postcards. Five warehouses and barns and adjoining fields full of tents are crammed full of antiques from every state. Antiques are *not previewed by dealers*—consumers are given equal access to the acres of antiques. Admission is $3, parking free, (313) 662-9453 for information.

# KALAMAZOO TO SOUTH HAVEN AND CHICAGO

Take a break in Kalamazoo en route to South Haven and Chicago. Arrive at the Idler Riverboat in South Haven for an early lunch. The Idler is one of the best places to relax in South Haven, and it's the perfect spot to start celebrating the final leg of your 22 Days trip. Blessed with some sunshine, North Beach provides ample room for sunbathing, play, and beachcombing. South Haven's outstanding B&Bs will make it very tempting to stay overnight unless you have a flight to catch or must be back in Chicago tonight. After taking advantage of the magnificent Lake Michigan shoreline, have dinner at one of Michigan's most enjoyable waterside restaurants.

## Suggested Schedule

| | |
|---|---|
| 8:00 a.m. | Breakfast in Ann Arbor. |
| 9:00 a.m. | Leave for Kalamazoo. |
| 11:00 a.m. | Visit Paw Paw's wineries. |
| 11:30 a.m. | Drive to South Haven. |
| 12:30 p.m. | Leisurely lunch on the Idler's deck. |
| 2:00 p.m. | North Beach recreation. |
| 4:30 p.m. | Three Pelican Restaurant's deck. |
| 5:30 p.m. | Dinner in South Haven. |
| 7:00 p.m. | Sunset stroll on beach. |
| 7:30 p.m. | Drive back to Chicago. |
| 10:00 p.m. | Arrive in downtown Chicago or at Midway or O'Hare Airport. |

**Travel Route: Ann Arbor to Chicago (271 miles)**
It's a smooth hour and a half (98 miles) on I-94 from Ann Arbor to Kalamazoo and another 38 miles to South Haven. After a brief sightseeing break in Kalamazoo, take M-43 to South Haven. Cross I-196, continue on Baily Avenue, Phillips, and Broadway to Dyckman. Williams Street and The Idler are on your left before crossing the

bridge to the north shore and North Beach, where you'll spend the afternoon and early evening.

Unless it's Sunday night, you shouldn't encounter much heavy traffic on I-94/I-90 into Chicago. Book your flight out of Chicago as late as possible in the evening to avoid 4:00 to 7:00 p.m. rush hour traffic in Chicago and to have a full vacation day. If you have to return your rented car before a flight, allow at least an hour at O'Hare and 45 minutes at Midway to get to your airplane.

### Sightseeing Highlights
▲▲ **Wineries in Paw Paw**—En route to South Haven, take M-40 south from M-43 to visit three wineries: St. Julian Winery, Frontenac Vineyards, and Warner Vineyards (watch for the signs). All of the wineries are open 9:00 a.m. to 5:00 p.m. weekdays and noon to 5:00 p.m. on Sundays. Paw Paw and Kalamazoo have a four-day Michigan Wine and Harvest Festival celebration annually on the first weekend after Labor Day, with wine and juice tasting, grape stomping, winery tours, carnival activities, arts and crafts shows, bike tours, and more.

▲ **Wolf Lake Hatchery, the Michigan Fisheries Interpretive Center**—Continue on M-43 to a fascinating place to observe state-of-the-art fish rearing ponds. Also see more than 100 different kinds of fishing gear. This fishery is unsurpassed in the Great Lakes for fishing experts and novices. Farther on M-43, in season pick blueberries at Frank Kovides' farm.

### Food
**The Magnolia Grille** in the **Idler Riverboat**, 515 Williams Street, in South Haven, (616) 637-8435, is the choice either for light fare in the open air on the Idler deck or for formal dining downstairs. A perfect day of dining is lunch at the Idler, an afternoon at the beach, and dinner at the new **Three Pelican Restaurant** (616) 637-5123), preceded by refreshments on the Three Pelican's deck. The Three Pelican is in South Haven at the end of N. Shore Drive, across the street from the North

Beach Inn, and under the same ownership as the Idler. Make reservations.

**Miller's Country House** in Union Pier, (616) 469-5950, on Route 12 just off I-94 at Union Pier Exit 6 or New Buffalo Exit 48, has the best food between South Haven and Chicago. If you're not ready for dinner in South Haven, I can't think of a better place for a marvelous last dinner before driving to Chicago. Make reservations.

# INDEX

# Other Books from John Muir Publications

**Adventure Vacations: From Trekking in New Guinea to Swimming in Siberia,** Richard Bangs (65-76-9) 256 pp. $17.95

**Asia Through the Back Door, 3rd ed.,** Rick Steves and John Gottberg (65-48-3) 326 pp. $15.95

**Being a Father: Family, Work, and Self,** *Mothering* Magazine (65-69-6) 176 pp. $12.95

**Buddhist America: Centers, Retreats, Practices,** Don Morreale (28-94-X) 400 pp. $12.95

**Bus Touring: Charter Vacations, U.S.A.,** Stuart Warren with Douglas Bloch (28-95-8) 168 pp. $9.95

**California Public Gardens: A Visitor's Guide,** Eric Sigg (65-56-4) 304 pp. $16.95 (Available 3/91)

**Catholic America: Self-Renewal Centers and Retreats,** Patricia Christian-Meyer (65-20-3) 325 pp. $13.95

**Complete Guide to Bed & Breakfasts, Inns & Guesthouses,** Pamela Lanier (65-43-2) 520 pp. $15.95

**Costa Rica: A Natural Destination,** Ree Strange Sheck (65-51-3) 280 pp. $15.95

**Elderhostels: The Students' Choice,** Mildred Hyman (65-28-9) 224 pp. $12.95 (2nd ed. available 5/91 $15.95)

**Environmental Vacations: Volunteer Projects to Save the Planet,** Stephanie Ocko (65-78-5) 240 pp. $14.95

**Europe 101: History & Art for the Traveler, 4th ed.,** Rick Steves and Gene Openshaw (65-79-3) 372 pp. $15.95

**Europe Through the Back Door, 9th ed.,** Rick Steves (65-42-4) 432 pp. $16.95

**Floating Vacations: River, Lake, and Ocean Adventures,** Michael White (65-32-7) 256 pp. $17.95

**Gypsying After 40: A Guide to Adventure and Self-Discovery,** Bob Harris (28-71-0) 264 pp. $14.95

**The Heart of Jerusalem,** Arlynn Nellhaus (28-79-6) 336 pp. $12.95

**Indian America: A Traveler's Companion,** Eagle/Walking Turtle (65-29-7) 424 pp. $16.95 (2nd ed. available 7/91 $16.95)

**Mona Winks: Self-Guided Tours of Europe's Top Museums,** Rick Steves and Gene Openshaw (28-85-0) 456 pp. $14.95

**Opera! The Guide to Western Europe's Great Houses,** Karyl Lynn Zietz (65-81-5) 280 pp. $18.95 (Available 4/91)

**Paintbrushes and Pistols: How the Taos Artists Sold the West,** Sherry C. Taggett and Ted Schwarz (65-65-3) 280 pp. $17.95

**The People's Guide to Mexico, 8th ed.,** Carl Franz (65-60-2) 608 pp. $17.95

**The People's Guide to RV Camping in Mexico,** Carl Franz with Steve Rogers (28-91-5) 320 pp. $13.95

**Preconception: A Woman's Guide to Preparing for Pregnancy and Parenthood,** Brenda E. Aikey-Keller (65-44-0) 232 pp. $14.95

**Ranch Vacations: The Complete Guide to Guest and Resort, Fly-Fishing, and Cross-Country Skiing Ranches,** Eugene Kilgore (65-30-0) 392 pp. $18.95 (2nd ed. available 5/91 $18.95)

**Schooling at Home: Parents, Kids, and Learning,** *Mothering* Magazine (65-52-1) 264 pp. $14.95

**The Shopper's Guide to Art and Crafts in the Hawaiian Islands,** Arnold Schuchter (65-61-0) 272 pp. $13.95

**The Shopper's Guide to Mexico,** Steve Rogers and Tina Rosa (28-90-7) 224 pp. $9.95

**Ski Tech's Guide to Equipment, Skiwear, and Accessories,** edited by Bill Tanler (65-45-9) 144 pp. $11.95

**Ski Tech's Guide to Maintenance and Repair,** edited by Bill Tanler (65-46-7) 160 pp. $11.95

**Teens: A Fresh Look,** *Mothering* Magazine (65-54-8) 240 pp. $14.95 (Available 3/91)

**A Traveler's Guide to Asian Culture,** Kevin Chambers (65-14-9) 224 pp. $13.95

**Traveler's Guide to Healing Centers and Retreats in North America,** Martine Rudee and Jonathan Blease (65-15-7) 240 pp. $11.95

**Understanding Europeans,** Stuart Miller (65-77-7) 272 pp. $14.95

**Undiscovered Islands of the Caribbean, 2nd ed.,** Burl Willes (65-55-6) 232 pp. $14.95

**Undiscovered Islands of the Mediterranean,** Linda Lancione Moyer and Burl Willes (65-53-X) 232 pp. $14.95

**A Viewer's Guide to Art: A Glossary of Gods, People, and Creatures,** Marvin S. Shaw and Richard Warren (65-66-1) 152 pp. $10.95 (Available 3/91)

## 2 to 22 Days Series

These pocket-size itineraries ($4\frac{1}{2}'' \times 8''$) are a refreshing departure from ordinary guidebooks. Each offers 22 flexible daily itineraries that can be used to get the most out of vacations of any length. Included are not only "must see" attractions but also little-known villages and hidden "jewels" as well as valuable general information.

**22 Days Around the World,** Roger Rapoport and Burl Willes (65-31-9) 200 pp. $9.95 (1992 ed. available 8/91 $11.95)

**2 to 22 Days Around the Great Lakes, 1991 ed.,** Arnold Schuchter (65-62-9) 176 pp. $9.95

**22 Days in Alaska,** Pamela Lanier (28-68-0) 128 pp. $7.95

**22 Days in the American Southwest, 2nd ed.,** Richard Harris (28-88-5) 176 pp. $9.95

**22 Days in Asia,** Roger Rapoport and Burl Willes (65-17-3) 136 pp. $7.95 (1992 ed. available 8/91 $9.95)

**22 Days in Australia, 3rd ed.,** John Gottberg (65-40-8) 148 pp. $7.95 (1992 ed. available 8/91 $9.95)

**22 Days in California, 2nd ed.,** Roger Rapoport (65-64-5) 176 pp. $9.95

**22 Days in China,** Gaylon Duke and Zenia Victor (28-72-9) 144 pp. $7.95

**22 Days in Europe, 5th ed.,** Rick Steves (65-63-7) 192 pp. $9.95

**22 Days in Florida,** Richard Harris (65-27-0) 136 pp. $7.95 (1992 ed. available 8/91 $9.95)

**22 Days in France,** Rick Steves (65-07-6) 154 pp. $7.95 (1991 ed. available 4/91 $9.95)

**22 Days in Germany, Austria & Switzerland, 3rd ed.,** Rick Steves (65-39-4) 136 pp. $7.95

**22 Days in Great Britain, 3rd ed.,** Rick Steves (65-38-6) 144 pp. $7.95 (1991 ed. available 4/91 $9.95)

**22 Days in Hawaii, 2nd ed.,** Arnold Schuchter (65-50-5) 144 pp. $7.95 (1992 ed. available 8/91 $9.95)

**22 Days in India,** Anurag Mathur (28-87-7) 136 pp. $7.95

**22 Days in Japan,** David Old (28-73-7) 136 pp. $7.95

**22 Days in Mexico, 2nd ed.,** Steve Rogers and Tina Rosa (65-41-6) 128 pp. $7.95

**22 Days in New England,** Anne Wright (28-96-6) 128 pp. $7.95 (1991 ed. available 4/91 $9.95)

**2 to 22 Days in New Zealand, 1991 ed.,** Arnold Schuchter (65-58-0) 176 pp. $9.95

**22 Days in Norway, Sweden, & Denmark,** Rick Steves (28-83-4) 136 pp. $7.95 (1991 ed. available 4/91 $9.95)

**22 Days in the Pacific Northwest,** Richard Harris (28-97-4) 136 pp. $7.95 (1991 ed. available 4/91 $9.95)

**22 Days in the Rockies,** Roger Rapoport (65-68-8) 176 pp. $9.95

**22 Days in Spain & Portugal, 3rd ed.,** Rick Steves (65-06-8) 136 pp. $7.95

**22 Days in Texas,** Richard Harris (65-47-5) 176 pp. $9.95

**22 Days in Thailand,** Derk Richardson (65-57-2) 176 pp. $9.95

**22 Days in the West Indies,** Cyndy & Sam Morreale (28-74-5)136 pp. $7.95

## "Kidding Around" Travel Guides for Young Readers

Written for kids eight years of age and older. Generously illustrated in two colors with imaginative characters and images. An adventure to read and a treasure to keep.

**Kidding Around Atlanta,** Anne Pedersen (65-35-1) 64 pp. $9.95

**Kidding Around Boston,** Helen Byers (65-36-X) 64 pp. $9.95

**Kidding Around Chicago,** Lauren Davis (65-70-X) 64 pp. $9.95

**Kidding Around the Hawaiian Islands,** Sarah Lovett (65-37-8) 64 pp. $9.95

**Kidding Around London,** Sarah Lovett (65-24-6) 64 pp. $9.95

**Kidding Around Los Angeles,** Judy Cash (65-34-3) 64 pp. $9.95

**Kidding Around the National Parks of the Southwest,** Sarah Lovett 108 pp. $12.95

**Kidding Around New York City,** Sarah Lovett (65-33-5) 64 pp. $9.95
**Kidding Around Paris,** Rebecca Clay (65-82-3) 64 pp. $9.95 (Available 4/91)
**Kidding Around Philadelphia,** Rebecca Clay (65-71-8) 64 pp. $9.95
**Kidding Around San Francisco,** Rosemary Zibart (65-23-8) 64 pp. $9.95
**Kidding Around Santa Fe,** Susan York (65-99-8) 64 pp. $9.95 (Available 5/91)
**Kidding Around Seattle,** Rick Steves (65-84-X) 64 pp. $9.95 (Available 4/91)
**Kidding Around Washington, D.C.,** Anne Pedersen (65-25-4) 64 pp. $9.95

## Environmental Books for Young Readers

Written for kids eight years and older. Examines the environmental issues and opportunities that today's kids will face during their lives.

**The Indian Way: Learning to Communicate with Mother Earth,** Gary McLain (65-73-4) 114 pp. $9.95
**The Kids' Environment Book: What's Awry and Why,** Anne Pedersen (55-74-2) 192 pp. $13.95
**No Vacancy: The Kids' Guide to Population and the Environment,** Glenna Boyd (61-000-7) 64 pp. $9.95 (Available 8/91)
**Rads, Ergs, and Cheeseburgers: The Kids' Guide to Energy and the Environment,** Bill Yanda (65-75-0) 108 pp. $12.95

## "Extremely Weird" Series for Young Readers

Written for kids eight years of age and older. Designed to help kids appreciate the world around them. Each book includes full-color photographs with detailed and entertaining descriptions of the "extremely weird" creatures.

**Extremely Weird Bats,** Sarah Lovett (61-008-2) 48 pp. $9.95 paper (Available 7/91)
**Extremely Weird Frogs,** Sarah Lovett (61-006-6) 48 pp. $9.95 paper (Available 6/91)
**Extremely Weird Spiders,** Sarah Lovett (61-007-4) 48 pp. $9.95 paper (Available 6/91)

## Automotive Repair Manuals

**How to Keep Your VW Alive, 14th ed.,** (65-80-7) 440 pp. $19.95
**How to Keep Your Subaru Alive** (65-11-4) 480 pp. $19.95
**How to Keep Your Toyota Pickup Alive** (28-81-3) 392 pp. $19.95
**How to Keep Your Datsun/Nissan Alive** (28-65-6) 544 pp. $19.95

## Other Automotive Books

**The Greaseless Guide to Car Care Confidence: Take the Terror Out of Talking to Your Mechanic,** Mary Jackson (65-19-X) 224 pp. $14.95

**Off-Road Emergency Repair & Survival,** James Ristow (65-26-2) 160 pp. $9.95

## Ordering Information

If you cannot find our books in your local bookstore, you can order directly from us. Please check the "Available" date above. If you send us money for a book not yet available, we will hold your money until we can ship you the book. Your books will be sent to you via UPS (for U.S. destinations). UPS will not deliver to a P.O. Box; please give us a street address. Include $2.75 for the first item ordered and $.50 for each additional item to cover shipping and handling costs. For airmail within the U.S., enclose $4.00. All foreign orders will be shipped surface rate; please enclose $3.00 for the first item and $1.00 for each additional item. Please inquire about foreign airmail rates.

## Method of Payment

Your order may be paid by check, money order, or credit card. We cannot be responsible for cash sent through the mail. All payments must be made in U.S. dollars drawn on a U.S. bank. Canadian postal money orders in U.S. dollars are acceptable. For VISA, MasterCard, or American Express orders, include your card number, expiration date, and your signature, or call (800) 888-7504. Books ordered on American Express cards can be shipped only to the billing address of the cardholder. Sorry, no C.O.D.'s. Residents of sunny New Mexico, add 5.875% tax to the total.

Address all orders and inquiries to:
John Muir Publications
P.O. Box 613
Santa Fe, NM 87504
(505) 982-4078
**(800) 888-7504**